Changing the
WORLD

One Relationship at a Time

*Focused Listening for Mutual
Support & Empowerment*

by Sheryl Karas, M.A.

**THE CROSSING PRESS
FREEDOM, CALIFORNIA**

For information on bulk purchases or group discounts for this and other Crossing Press titles, please contact our Special Sales Manager at 800-777-1048.

Visit our Web site on the Internet: www.crossingpress.com

Disclaimer:
The ideas, suggestions, and techniques in this book are not intended to be a substitute for professional mental health care. Anyone with a history of serious mental illness should consult a licensed therapist or psychiatrist.

Library of Congress Cataloging-in-Publication Data

Karas, Sheryl, 1958-
    Changing the world one relationship at a time: focused listening
for mutual support & empowerment / by Sheryl Karas.
        p. cm. -- (Personal power)
    Includes bibliographical references.
    ISBN 0-89594-945-8 (pbk.)
    1. Listening. 2. Interpersonal communication. 3. Interpersonal.
relations. I. Title. II. Series.
BF323.L5K37   1998
158--dc21   98-24641
                                                              CIP

To All My Communities

Acknowledgments

I almost let this book go without any acknowledgments. Since the material presented here was fifteen years in the making there are so many people to thank and so many people I might inadvertently leave out that it seemed too daunting a task. But I don't exist in a vacuum and I am grateful to all the aspects of my life and the people in it who brought me to this stage in my development. In particular I wish to acknowledge the Re-Evaluation Counseling Community and my friends who paved the way for me to get involved in this organization. They taught me there was some value in being willing to look at my past as I proceeded to create the life I wished to have. They helped me reclaim my ability to cry and to move on with renewed strength and courage. I also wish to thank my dear friends who would have NOTHING to do with this process for reminding me of the value of being who I am without excessive self-improvement, and for teaching me the importance of emotional boundaries and inner stability. They helped me distill my thinking and create a gentler, more spiritually-attuned model of reciprocal peer support. To that end, I would also like to thank my teachers and classmates at the Institute of Transpersonal Psychology, my spiritual guides, and the other writers and communicators of spiritual and emotional guidance that I have learned from over the years. I am grateful that there are many other people who are willing to share their experience as they proceed on their own journeys. Last, but not least, I would like to thank Elaine Gill and all the people at *The Crossing Press* for believing in me enough to take a chance on publishing this book. Namasté.

Contents

Introduction

According to most scientists and environmentalists the world is on the edge of ecological disaster. The hole in the ozone layer is growing, forests are disappearing, deserts are spreading, water supplies are being contaminated, and the world population keeps increasing. That alone is daunting enough, but add to that the problems of war, poverty, crime, AIDS, and other infectious diseases, and throw in issues of sexism, racism, classism, and homophobia and it is easy to understand why many people shy away from the topic of social change. It feels overwhelming. Can the efforts of one person even begin to make a difference? And besides, you might say, I'm struggling enough to make a living and raise a family—how would I possibly have anything left to change the world?

Well, what if it were possible to own a set of tools designed to make your life easier, saner, and more fun? And what if it were possible that by using those tools you would be helping someone else make a significant improvement in their lives at the same time? And taking the fantasy even further, what if you could use these tools in a larger arena by joining forces to create change on a community-wide level or beyond? Would that make a difference? I think it would!

Such tools exist. The key lies in building strong, supportive relationships and communities, something we all say we want but often feel at a loss to create. This book is about how to create partnerships and alliances that have the power to change the world. Starting with a few simple techniques, you and a friend can learn to empower and support each other to take charge of your lives and go after your dreams. You can use these skills to communicate better with lovers, family, friends, or co-workers, and to create groups flexible and creative enough to solve any problem you can imagine.

The main tool I'll be emphasizing is the ability to work with emotions. Because our society tends to delegate the emotional realm to the hands of professionals, many of us lack the skills and confidence to be in charge of our emotional lives. This leaves us open to exploitation and manipulation by the very social forces we might wish to change. It also keeps us dependent on professional services that are expensive and increasingly unavailable through insurance and health maintenance programs.

You should understand that this is not another self-help book geared towards personal growth. Unlike psychotherapy, which tends to encourage people to focus exclusively on inner work and individual development, the approach we'll be using does not separate the individual from the social system. Traditional psychotherapy says your problems are your fault or your family's fault. If you have trouble fitting into society, if you're not productive or successful by society's standards, if you *are* successful but feel unhappy anyway, there's something wrong with you. Forget about what's wrong with society.

I don't agree. The psychiatric community would have us believe that up to 90 percent of our families are dysfunctional. If our society was constructed in ways that truly supported family systems, is it possible that the rate of dysfunction would really be so high? By focusing on individuals and families as separate from the communities they grew up in, I believe our current mental health system bypasses the root of the problems it seeks to address and leaves people less empowered to make the changes that really need to happen.

I expect to be challenging some of your assumptions about yourself and how the world works. As you read this book I hope you will question what I say and try out my suggestions before deciding that they will or will not work for you. In fact, for this information to be truly beneficial it needs to be experienced, not just read about. Call up a friend and read it together. Do the exercises together and come to your own conclusions.

An acquaintance of mine says that one person CAN change the world if she thinks of herself as a leader and empowers other people to become leaders, too. Are you capable of being a leader? If you're like most people, you don't think so. Most people think of leaders as the star quarterback on their favorite football team or as the president or prime minister of an entire nation. We rarely think of ordinary people living ordinary lives as being leaders, but I see ordinary people just like you and me doing extraordinary things with their lives everyday. I'm banking on the belief that by the time you finish working with this book, you'll see yourself differently and will have the tools and resources to put your leadership potential into action, at least in your own household. And because each person touches the lives of so many others, that change alone will make a difference.

The Balanced Wheel

"Your health is bound to be affected if, day after day, you say the opposite of what you feel, if you grovel before what you dislike and rejoice at what brings you nothing but misfortune."

BORIS PASTERNAK

I like to think of the human being as a bicycle wheel. To spin smoothly and work dependably, a bicycle wheel needs to be balanced—that means all the spokes must have the same amount of tension to keep the wheel in as perfect a circle as possible. If a human being were a bicycle wheel, all aspects of his or her life would be in place and in balance. Those aspects include the intellectual (beliefs about the world, self and others, decision-making ability, logic and intuition, creativity and problem solving), the physical (exercise and play, rest and relaxation, nutrition, touch and physical affection), the emotional (love and kindness, joy and peace, grief, anger, fear, desire and drive), and the transpersonal (connections that go beyond the physical self: relationships with other people, family, the greater community, nature, the universe, God and/or an inner Higher Power).

Now let's picture an unbalanced wheel. (See diagrams on page 12.) Suppose there was a lump of lead on this bicycle tire. The wheel can still turn and take us where we want to go, but the ride will be more bumpy. It will take more energy to get there, and eventually the stress and strain on the wheel will cause the spokes to loosen or pull away, causing the entire wheel to eventually fall apart.

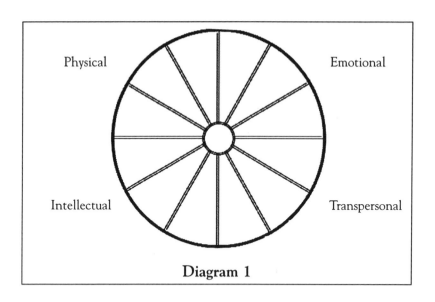

Physical

Emotional

Intellectual

Transpersonal

Diagram 1

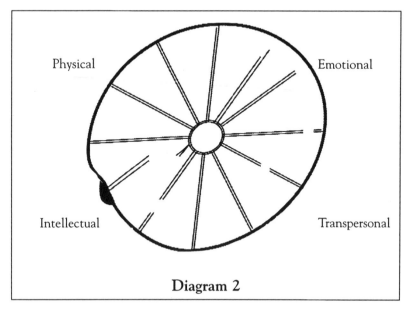

Physical

Emotional

Intellectual

Transpersonal

Diagram 2

Like a bicycle wheel, an imbalance in a human being that is left unchecked will create havoc in every aspect of the system.

Western culture emphasizes the development of body and mind, but our emotional and transpersonal lives are severely underdeveloped. People in the United States are starved for community and often must struggle to create and maintain adequate personal relationships. We're also trained to severely control our emotions, and because of this we have a lot of unreleased emotional tension that acts like the lead on that tire. Let me give you an example.

Years ago a teacher told me that it took more energy to keep from crying than it did to cry, and I didn't believe her. For me, crying, especially in front of another person, felt too humiliating to bear except in the most extreme circumstances. I took the strong silent approach to dealing with emotional upset and prided myself on my self-control.

But then I got to know a three-year-old and his mother. One day we were riding in a car, and the little boy was tired and upset because his older sibling was harassing him. Finally, he reached his limit and began to cry. His mom immediately insisted that he stop. I said the crying didn't bother me, but she said it did bother most people, so he had to learn to stop it. She threatened to take something he really wanted away from him if he didn't control himself. And control himself he did. This is what it took:

He tensed every muscle in his little body. He held his breath, gritted his teeth, made his hands into fists, and rocked back and forth hitting himself. His mom couldn't see him because she was driving. She said, "Now there's a big boy. Doesn't that feel much better?" The little boy shook his head "no" but couldn't say so out loud because he was trying so hard to keep from crying.

If this situation were repeated often enough, eventually his physical reactions would become second nature. We all hold our breath, clench our jaws, and tense our muscles, but we don't notice ourselves doing so anymore. We stop noticing the effort it takes to hold back our tears because it seems normal. I can't imagine a baby who wouldn't cry when it was hurting, but big boys and girls do it all the time. We're used to it. Meanwhile, the physical tension this involves takes its toll in headaches, inflexible bodies, ulcers, asthma attacks, heart disease, and cancer.

It also affects our relationships. It's hard for many people to have close, loving, and committed relationships, because that means being vulnerable enough to risk feeling grief should our loved ones hurt us, leave, or die. Grief is the most painful emotion we can feel. If the ability to release emotion is blocked, the pain of the grief we carry and the efforts we make to prevent ourselves from feeling that pain can be extremely debilitating. A person who has been trained not to cry or feel often carries a heavy load of unreleased pain from past experiences and feels the need to protect him- or herself by avoiding situations that might trigger that pain. With a percentage of one's mental ability focused in such a way, one's ability to think clearly and make rational, loving decisions is affected. The way one perceives the world is changed—through the lens of fear the most wonderful opportunities for love and connection can seem fraught with danger. On the transpersonal level, the ability to create and maintain healthy communities is damaged, since all communities are made up of relationships between people.

People in our society express admiration for people who exhibit stoic self-control, and discomfort or even disgust for someone who falls apart. As I write this, the funeral for Princess Diana has just taken place. A news report I heard yesterday said that Diana would be proud at how well her boys hid their tears. I thought it was sad that they felt they had to hold back their tears at the funeral. Suppressing tears seems to be a trifling problem at first glance, one we don't even question. Yet it is clear to me that, because our society is made up of relationships and our emotional health affects the quality of the relationships we create, a significant imbalance in just this one aspect of a person's life can have unwanted consequences that go far beyond the individual.

So what can we do about this? How can we raise emotionally healthy children in a society that prohibits emotional expression? How can we rebalance our own lives after a lifetime of such conditioning?

We start by listening.

Listening with All Your Senses

*"Unless you listen, you can't know anybody. Oh, you will know
facts and what is in the newspapers and all of history, perhaps,
but you will not know one single person. You know, I have
come to think listening is love, that's what it really is."*

BRENDA UELAND

I know a woman who went to the hospital for major surgery. She
complained to me that when her friends visited they would all
launch into their own stories about hospitals and surgery whenever
she would try to tell them about her worries. Instead of getting the
support she desperately needed, she felt more alone than ever, and
even more frightened because of their horror stories. This is a very
common experience, typical of what happens when people confine
themselves to ordinary conversation patterns. Someone tells a story
and someone else tells about a similar experience, which leads to
another story and another. There's nothing wrong with this—we
build connections with one another through exploring common
interests and experiences. Unfortunately, we can be so wrapped up
in what someone else's story reminds us of and in our desire to tell
our own story that we can't be with each other in more than a superficial way. In times of crisis this level of interaction becomes painful.
That's when we need closeness and an emotional anchor to comfort
and steady us, which we don't get from casual conversation.

We also need a deeper level of listening when we are in a conflict with someone or attempting to interact with a person from a dif-

ferent cultural background. White, middle-class Americans like to assume that despite superficial differences, all people are basically the same. We say things like, "I don't see the color of your skin" or, "I don't care what your religion is." But the fact is that race, class, culture, gender, age, and sexual orientation create different experiences for people, which in turn, shape our world views. We might share the same biological functions, but we don't see the world the same way. The same experience can have a very different meaning to two people. To bridge those differences, we need better listening skills.

BASIC TRAINING IN ATTENTIVE LISTENING

Better listening skills are within everyone's grasp, and you can start right now. This is a section for doing, not just reading. You need a partner, about ten minutes of time, and a clock or timer. Choose one person to be the listener. That person will be paying complete attention to the other person for five minutes. When the time is up, switch roles.

When it is your turn to listen, I'd like you to pretend you can't talk. Visualize tape over your mouth or bite your tongue—whatever it takes to remind yourself not to speak. Let go of your need to say the right thing. For this exercise there is nothing to say and nothing to do besides pay attention with all your senses.

Consider that you have a unique opportunity to get to know your friend in a deeper way than you have in the past and to know something about his or her experience of living in the world that is very important for you to understand. Even if he or she chooses to remain silent, information will be communicated to you if you pay attention. Tell yourself that at his or her core your friend has a spirit that is completely lovable, loving, intelligent, creative, powerful, and happy to be alive. Anything else you see is an indication of tension or pain left over from hurtful past experiences. Allow the natural love and delight you would have for such a wonderful human being to show in your facial expression and in your touch. Make eye contact and hold hands with your partner if it is comfortable for both of you (there may be cultural or emotional issues that make this inappropriate).

As you pay attention, listen with your ears, but don't just listen to what your friend says. Listen to the choice of words, how they are said, and with what tone of voice. The pitch and loudness of a person's voice says something as well as the speed. But that's not all. Listen with your eyes. Does your friend look relaxed, confident, and powerful? Or do you see a furrowed brow, a clenched jaw, or hunched shoulders? Also listen with your body. If you are holding hands, notice whether they are hot or cold, trembling or sweating. Notice if that changes at any particular time. If your attention drifts away into daydreams, related memories, or personal problems, simply bring yourself back to the present moment and resume listening to your friend.

If you are the person receiving the attention, there is nothing you need to do. You may use the time any way you like. You may want to talk about what it is like to have someone pay attention to you like this or what your day was like. Is there something on your mind, something you'd like your friend to know? Or would you rather remain silent? You don't need to talk, but do take a moment to notice how you are feeling physically and emotionally and any thoughts you are having. It may be useful to share that information, but there is no requirement.

When you are receiving attention after having been the listener, please do not refer to anything your friend said. If something he or she said brought up your own memories or feelings, share this if you like, but do not comment on his or her experience in any way. Focus on your own experience.

When both of you have had a chance to give and receive attention, share what it was like to do this exercise. Did you prefer giving or receiving? What did you like and dislike about each role? Places of discomfort will indicate where your growth may begin. In my classes, I find that most people are surprised to discover how thoroughly they have been trained not to be in these roles.

Some people find the previous exercise to be very moving. Many have never had anyone pay such complete attention to them. Just being looked at in a loving way can be a powerful experience.

Other people find the attention embarrassing or anxiety-producing. "What are they thinking about me?" "Am I doing this right?" Because it is likely that some feelings will be stirred up, in the next chapter we'll discuss emotions and how to work with them.

mirror dancing

Mirror dancing is a fun way to communicate nonverbally with another human being.

1. Start by facing your partner, with your hands facing each other's about 2–6 inches away. Make eye contact and dance, moving your hands to the music, following your partner's hands as closely as possible. After about 5 minutes or more, share what that experience was like.

2. Choose a completely different piece of music, something with a different tempo or emotional quality. Repeat the same exercise as above.

Notice that the instructions do not designate one person as leader and the other as follower. Did you tend to slip into one role or the other? Was it hard to keep eye contact and still follow what your partner was doing? How did the choice of music affect your experience?

When I did this exercise the first time, I found myself following my partner in movement that was physically uncomfortable for me. I eventually realized that I could change this experience by leading and allowing my partner to follow me. To my amazement, my partner reported afterward having the same thoughts and feelings! He decided to change the movement in exactly the same way at exactly the same time that I did. So who really was leading and who was following and who actually made the decision to change the movement?

(continued)

mirror dancing (continued)

Variation

I. In a group, dance freeform to music of any kind. Dance your own dance, keeping your eyes closed if that helps. Then open your eyes and continue dancing. When you feel ready, look around and find someone whose dance looks interesting to you. Copy their movements as closely as possible and make eye contact. After a few minutes, move on and find another partner to mirror dance with.

This is a great way to experience another person's way of being for a brief period of time. It is especially informative to try dancing a dance that is completely foreign to you. It's also a great flirting technique!

Working with Emotions

*"Stormclouds finally weep, because the lightning
has started to laugh. With heavy tears everywhere
coming down, the fields get uncontrollably tickled."*

RUMI

We're all born with a natural ability to heal. If we cut our finger, the blood clots and the cut mends. We don't have to do anything—it happens by itself. The same is true for emotional hurts. When a baby feels bad, it cries or screams or trembles or kicks its feet. Nobody teaches the baby to do this. It is natural to release emotion in a physical way because emotion in many respects is a physical process.

There have been many studies over the last few years investigating what's happening in the body during emotional arousal and catharsis. The picture isn't complete, but there have been some interesting findings with accompanying theories. For example, experimenters have analyzed the chemical composition of tears shed as a result of strong emotions and those shed as a reaction to the smell of onions. They have also analyzed nervous perspiration and perspiration resulting from exposure to heat. Emotionally related tears and sweat both contain stress hormones that are not found in the other type of tears and sweat. Some people theorize that we cry when we are sad and sweat when we are nervous to rid the body of these chemicals. The same may be true for the trembling that most of us associate with intense fear.

A friend once told me that he no longer believes that trembling means he is experiencing fear. Now he sees it as his power moving through. I loved that and have used it with my listening partners ever since. Not only is it a positive reframing of what most people label a negative sensation, it's also pretty close to the truth of what's happening on the physical level. There's a part of our nervous system that scientists call the autonomic nervous system. It controls a lot of the automatic things we depend on our bodies to do. It is made up of two parts—the sympathetic nervous system and the parasympathetic system. The sympathetic nervous system is our emergency response network. It increases our heart rates and our breathing by releasing adrenaline and other chemicals into the blood stream in response to any call to action, especially the perception of danger. Adrenaline is known as the fight or flight compound. It's responsible for the surge of energy we feel when we are driving and suddenly a small child darts out from between two parked cars directly in front of us. Our responses speed up, our senses become more acute, and our ability to act decisively with great agility or strength is heightened. We are literally flooded with power.

The parasympathetic nervous system is what kicks in when it is safe for the body to rest. It slows down the heart rate, slows the breathing, and allows us to feel calm. This is what should happen when the present moment is okay—when we do not hit the child and the crisis is over. However, the chemicals released by the sympathetic nervous system are still floating around in the body, telling it to speed up. A chemical reaction comes into play, which is more complex than we need to get into, but it appears that the combined activities of the parasympathetic and sympathetic systems cause the shaking, perspiring, and other forms of emotional release that typically occur at this time. The way I usually describe this is that when part of our attention is on the stressful thing that happened in the recent or distant past, and part of our attention is on the safety of the present moment, emotions we've been holding will automatically release unless there is a deliberate or habitual effort to control the process.

When the process of emotional catharsis is interrupted, the chemicals that would otherwise dissipate are stored in the body along with the memory of the hurtful experience and all our reactions. The feelings associated with these memories are triggered whenever something in our present environment is sufficiently similar to the stored experience. So, for example, when passing a lilac bush, you might be flooded with angry feelings and memories because you were treated badly by a relative who always wore lilac perfume. To avoid feeling these feelings, we develop unconscious patterns of behavior that are rigid or compulsive in nature—you might decide you hate the smell of lilacs or avoid the side of the street that the lilac bush is on without being aware of your unconscious motivation. This habit will tend to persist until new ways of thinking or acting are adopted and enough positive experiences are accumulated to counteract the effect of the negative memory. Releasing the old emotional memory considerably speeds this process along and helps make positive changes last. That's why most systems of emotional healing stress the importance of reviewing past experiences. However, deliberate reliving of past trauma is not necessary, and it is possible to work on that trauma without looking directly at past memories. Feelings can also be released through bodywork or certain breathing practices.

Emotional catharsis can take many forms. Tears, perspiration, and trembling have already been mentioned. Emotion is also released through laughter; angry vocalization and movement; animated, nonrepetitive talking; and yawning. Some people sense energy moving through their bodies, heat or cold, or tingling sensations. There may be a spontaneous urge to stretch or move the body in various ways. Increased kidney and bowel activity is also common.

USING FOCUSED LISTENING
FOR EMOTIONAL SUPPORT

What holds us back most from fulfilling our full potential and living happy, satisfying lives is the emotional baggage we carry, especially that which originated from hurtful situations repeated frequently or lived with constantly during some period of our lives. Usually, we're not even aware of the habitual feelings or rigid patterns we learned to accept because they are so much a part of our lives that we don't remember life being any other way. Fortunately, it is relatively simple for two people to help each other out of such difficulties. It takes attentive listening, persistence, and a mutual agreement to be of assistance.

The basic strategy we use is to create a balance of attention between the hurtful experiences of the past and the benign reality of the present moment. We do that right from the start of every listening session. Very few people were ever hurt by someone paying attention to them in a nonjudgmental, respectful, and loving way, so that's the kind of attention we provide. We create a present moment that is as close as possible to the opposite of the hurtful experiences. When we know the source of a person's difficulties, we can help the person even more by saying something that contradicts the hurtful messages or by encouraging the person to say or do something to actively combat that harmful conditioning.

How to Play a Counseling Role in a Focused Listening Session

When you listen to your partner during time set aside specifically for mutual listening, you are doing a type of peer counseling. Don't be frightened by the term "counseling"—you are not expected to be a therapist. You will simply be paying attention in a very specific way to help your friend sort out his or her difficulties. It takes practice, but if you follow these basic guidelines, you can't go wrong.

1. Settle yourself into a comfortable sitting position and then take a few deep breaths all the way down to your belly. Feel your feet on the floor and your rear-end on your chair and, as you feel the solidity of your body, remind yourself of your inherent value as a listener. You are completely good, loving, lovable, capable, intelligent, creative, and powerful. In other words, you have everything it takes to be a great peer counselor. Just your attentive, loving presence alone

(as we practiced in the last chapter) is enough to make a difference. Any worries or negative feelings you have about yourself are an indication of where you've been hurt, and you can attend to those feelings when it is your turn to receive attention. For the time being, allow your personal concerns to recede and remind yourself of your intention to be of assistance to your partner. This step shouldn't take long—after the habits of centering yourself and setting your intention are established, it will only take a minute or so to return to this state in future sessions.

If at any point during the session you find yourself getting flustered, confused, or identifying too strongly with your partner, break eye contact for just a second or two, take a deep breath, and return to this feeling of solidity and intention.

2. Remind yourself that your friend is inherently good, loving, lovable, capable, intelligent, etc. and that anything else you see is an indication of where he or she was hurt. What do you particularly love and appreciate about this person? Let yourself feel delighted with him or her and allow your feelings to show through a warm smile and appreciative gaze. Hold your friend's hand, if you are both comfortable with touch. Step 2 is 90 percent of what I do and all you really *need* to do besides pay attention.

3. Give your full attention to your friend and notice any behavior patterns and limiting belief systems that are inconsistent for a person with the qualities mentioned in Steps 1 and 2. Often this is as simple as asking your friend what holds her back and having her tell you. But even if your friend has no idea of what the core issue is, clear indications will be present in what a person says, how he or she says it, the tone of voice, facial expressions, or posture. These patterns and beliefs always come from earlier experiences, including societal conditioning.

4. Find a way to balance the misconceptions and rigid patterns you notice. For example, if your friend habitually puts himself down, you could tell him what you admire about him or ask him to say what he appreciates about himself. It can help to know what the underlying issues are so you can address the difficulty more precisely, but sometimes that information is not immediately accessible. Luckily, you don't *need* to know. Reversing the obvious patterns of behavior will work well enough. If you do and say the opposite of what the pattern does and says, and you do this sincerely, accurately, and persistently, the emotions that are keeping the patterns in place will bubble to the surface and any underlying issues will become obvious.

5. Allow and encourage any emotional release, and listen attentively to any insights that arise. Do not give any advice of your own or tell your own stories unless your partner asks. (Even then, be careful not to dominate your friend's time. Encourage him or her to come to his or her own solutions, and keep personal storytelling to an absolute minimum.)

6. If possible, help your friend formulate a strategy to reinforce the valuable aspects of the session by choosing a new way of acting in the world.

I've just described a formal way of providing peer-counseling assistance, but the main process involved is not much different from what we might naturally do for our friends. Let me give you an example.

A man and a woman are getting ready to go to a party. The woman has just spent an hour fussing with her hair. She finally announces, "I can't go! I hate my hair! I can't be seen in public like this!" She's having a classic "bad hair" day.

Clearly, there are some old feelings in the way because if she had not taken in some hurtful message about herself, she wouldn't be so extremely concerned about her appearance. Women in our society are pressured to look a certain way. The conditioning comes through women's magazines, movies, TV advertising, ridicule, parents who focused too much on appearance, etc. We don't know exactly what happened to this woman, but that doesn't matter. The patterns and limiting beliefs are plain to see: she is acting and talking as if she needs to limit her social life because her hair isn't curling in the right direction. The risk of rejection seems sky high. From our perspective this is obviously an illusion, but as almost any woman in our society can attest, when these emotions are triggered, the illusion feels very real indeed.

So we've identified the unhealthy pattern and belief system. The natural thing to do is to oppose the illusion and try to bring the person back to balance. In the above scenario the man might say, "What do you mean? Of course, you can go to the party. You look fine!"

Unfortunately, people believe that by pointing out the obvious the other person will automatically come to their senses and stop feeling so bad. Instead, the feelings are likely to come up even stronger. The woman might say something like, "How can you say that?! Just look at me!"

Now at this point most men try to give advice, or throw up their hands in resignation, or get angry, or feel like they said the wrong thing. But if the man decided to play a counseling role, he could put his arms around her, look at her lovingly, and in a loving voice say, "I would be proud to be seen with you anywhere."

If the woman continued to be upset, the man might encourage her to talk more about this situation. He would not try to convince her to stop feeling bad or voice any judgments about her being in the grip of this illusion in either words or tone of voice. Instead, he would listen and make a sincere attempt to understand her experience. He might acknowledge that anyone who grew up in similar conditions would feel the same way, but that she is wonderful just the way she is and doesn't need to put up with such limitations anymore. "You are a wonderful, valuable, interesting person, and anyone who would discount you or not want to get to know you because of the way your hair looks has a problem!" Or he could try a more playful approach. He could mess his own hair up and encourage her to do the same—"Let's make it look *really* bad! We could create a new style—go wild!"

Most women would respond to one of these approaches with laughter, tears, or some other form of emotional release. Usually, within just a few minutes, enough tension can be lifted for the illusion to lose its power. The woman might not be completely at ease, but more than likely she will feel more relaxed and lighter in attitude.

As you can see, you don't need to be Sigmund Freud to provide emotional assistance. This style of counseling is not about giving advice or analyzing each other's behavior. In fact that kind of interference often prevents a person from working things out for himself or herself—it can be an obstacle to empowerment. The hardest parts of peer counseling are the feelings that come up for you when a friend expresses strong emotions and in showing your love so openly and persistently. With practice it will feel much easier.

SETTING UP A LISTENING PARTNERSHIP

When I teach peer counseling, my students have the benefit of being in a class where they can see counseling demonstrations, practice the skills with feedback, ask questions, and experience being counseled. It is impossible to duplicate this experience in a book, but you can get a lot of value from setting up a regular time to experiment and practice with a friend.

Choose a time and place where you both will feel comfortable and will not be interrupted. Decide together how much time you would like to spend and then split the time. About 15–20 minutes each is a good place to start. If you find the experience useful, experiment with an arrangement that will be most beneficial for both of you—10 minutes each a day, a half-hour each twice a week, an hour each once a week—whatever you can fit in. One of you will give counseling attention and support while the other receives this attention. Then you will switch roles. It is important to take equal amounts of time to keep your relationship reciprocal and to counteract any perceived power imbalances (more on this in Chapter 7). Have a clock or timer nearby.

Before beginning, make an agreement that anything that is said during this special listening time will remain confidential. Confidentiality is a basic tool for creating a space safe enough for someone to reveal themselves to you on a deep level. It is also a good idea to agree not to talk to each other later on about what you hear during a session. Sometimes people need a time and place to bring up issues that are too difficult to talk about in casual conversation. You will have more success with this if you structure each session in such a way to set it apart from ordinary socializing time.

Having a ritual to open and close the session usually works well for this. The best kind of opening ritual will bring both of you fully into the present moment and allow you both to set your intentions for the session. For most people simply going through the process of deciding how much time to spend, setting a timer, and deciding who will receive attention first, plumping pillows, getting comfortable, and holding hands is ritual enough, but feel free to elaborate on this if you desire. A minimal closing ritual might be mutual thanks and appreciation for the attention just received, setting a date for your next listening session, and a hug.

Start and end each person's time by doing something that calls attention to positive aspects of his or her life or the present moment. When I'm playing the role of counselor I always ask my partner to begin by telling me anything that's been good since the last time we met, unless a current crisis makes this inappropriate. This question serves several purposes, which I will discuss in the next chapter. At the end of the session I always allow at least five minutes to help my partner focus on neutral or pleasant aspects of the present moment. We might do some stretching or yoga, go for a short walk, or do some simple gardening task. I might ask about various objects in the environment or provide a mind puzzle, riddle, or a guided meditation. The purpose of this interlude is to create a transition between the emotional involvement of the session and the rest of one's life. Stirred up emotions can sometimes be disruptive. It's important to develop the habit of being able to put these issues aside at will by redirecting one's attention.

The bulk of the session is spent on whatever the person receiving attention wishes to focus on. Many people have found that picking one issue and sticking with it for several weeks or months is very fruitful. Other people use the time to talk about whatever feels most stressful in the moment. The session could also be spent in goal-setting, thinking out loud about a project, or mapping out a strategy to reach one's goals. I've rehearsed class lectures in my sessions and have listened to other people perform songs they've just written or practice speeches. I've provided support for people writing resumes and filling out school and job applications. One person I know asked her listening partner to join her at the beach and provide counseling-style support while she got on a surfboard for the first time.

The ideal situation is for both participants to work together to help the one receiving attention. When you are the receiver, it is not your partner's job to fix you or tell you what to do. You are in charge of your own healing; she or he is just your assistant. So always tell your listening partner if something worked particularly well in a previous session or if you gained some insights from a dream or some other source. You can also help her fine-tune her counseling by telling her any thoughts you have about what might be helpful as the session progresses. Your partner's main role is to create a safe, loving environment for you to work on challenging issues that are difficult to work through alone.

COMMONLY ASKED QUESTIONS

From what you've said I imagine that releasing emotion is the goal of focused listening. Is that correct?

No. The goal is to understand each other and ourselves better. We develop awareness of our habitual patterns and can thus free our thinking and act more powerfully and flexibly. Reclaiming the ability to release feelings is very useful, but it is only one of many tools to help us get where we want to go; it is not the destination. I focus on emotional release in this book because when we challenge the deeply ingrained patterns and beliefs that are holding us back, feelings often bubble to the surface. Without having a way to handle those feelings, we often allow them to stop us from making the changes we desire in our lives.

I don't want to cry. It hurts!

Grief hurts. Crying, fully given in to, does not. Pain comes from the tension between holding back tears and letting them come through. Many of us as children were humiliated or rejected for crying, and some of us were threatened or hit ("Stop crying this instant or I'll give you something to cry about!"). If your past includes abuse of this nature, it can be very difficult to allow yourself to cry fully. Don't push it. There are other ways to release emotional tension.

Breathe deeply and ask yourself where you feel tension in your body. If you need to close your eyes to focus on your internal experience, go ahead. When I'm holding back emotion I usually feel tightness in my throat, jaw, or chest. You or your partner might gently but firmly touch the tight area. Then ask yourself (or have your partner ask) if you are willing to release the emotion you are experiencing in the most gentle way possible. If the answer is yes, continue to breathe and imagine the area as a tightly closed fist that is opening just a little bit at a time. When the area is relaxed enough, the form of physical or emotional release most appropriate for you will usually occur. Because you are consciously controlling the process by only opening as far as it feels comfortable, you can slow down or stop at any time.

I don't want my partner to cry!
I don't want him or her to feel bad!

Most of us have been trained to believe that tears are an indication of pain rather than the release of pain. We think that by interrupting the flow of tears the pain will stop. When you have had the opportunity to see or experience for yourself the relief that comes from *fully* releasing an emotional blockage, it will be easier to trust in the process.

Is emotional catharsis ever harmful?

Not usually, but there are circumstances in which it is not useful. Imagine a person hitting themselves with a hammer and then crying because it hurts. This happens more often than you might imagine. Crying while telling yourself, "I'm just no good," "I can't do anything right," "How could I be so stupid," "I'll never find anyone to love me," "It's all my fault," "It's my father's fault! I'd have the life I want if he hadn't…," etc. is like hitting yourself in the head with a hammer. In this case you are hurting yourself by reinforcing the negative messages you have been limited by. It can actually make the problem worse. Reviewing traumatic situations from your past without focusing on the capabilities and resources you have now is also problematic because it tends to reinforce the original experience. In the next chapter we'll focus on replacing negative programming with a more positive outlook.

walking in character

This exercise illustrates how our emotional state affects what we do with our bodies and how changing what we do physically can affect our emotional state. By trying on different characters we see how easily we identify with certain roles and attitudes and how, with awareness, we can change our experience at will. This information will help you recognize the physical manifestations of emotional imbalance and help you suggest or model a physical action that may restore your partner to a healthier state.

1. Walk about the room at whatever speed and in whatever way that feels comfortable for you.

2. Now imagine that you are a person who is trying to catch a plane and that you're late. Move about the room in that character's mode. Notice how you move in that role. What is your posture and facial expression like? How do you feel?

3. Now imagine that you are an angry, street-tough kid and walk as that character. Imagine how you look and notice how you move. How does that feel?

4. Imagine that you are 3-year-old child on a fun excursion. How are you moving? How do you feel?

5. Imagine that you are a person with a terrible problem, someone who is feeling hopeless and depressed. How are you moving now? How has your posture changed from the previous character?

6. Imagine you are a person who feels confident and relaxed, happy to be alive, and optimistic about the future. Again, notice how you're moving, holding your body, and how you feel.

Acting the part of a character can help to free your attention from almost any bad mood or energy drain. Use this technique any time you feel stuck and need a change of perspective.

Balancing the Wheel

How could anyone ever tell you
You were anything less than beautiful?
How could anyone ever tell you
You were less than whole?
How could anyone fail to notice
That your loving is a miracle?
How deeply you're connected to my soul.

SONG LYRICS BY LIBBY RODERICK

Ninety-nine percent of the people I meet have no trouble at all focusing on what's bad about their lives, what they're disappointed about, what causes them stress, or how badly they feel about themselves. I happen to be an expert at this myself. As I started writing this book I found myself listening to vicious imaginary critics who tore apart every sentence: "She's not being academic enough! Wasn't that slang? Where are her footnotes?" "That was a pretty simplistic explanation of neurophysiological functioning!" "Actually, I thought it was pretty boring. Why'd she waste so much space on that?" It went on and on. There were times when it was a miracle that I persisted in writing a book at all.

I have found that most people are equally expert at ripping down their self-esteem and preventing themselves from pursuing their hearts' desires. Why would we do this? If another person made the comments that I torture myself with, I'd be furious! I find myself wondering what benefit such behavior has for me. The thought that popped into my head was, that these criticisms keep me from risking humiliation and disappointment. If I don't finish this book, I will never have to hear such criticisms from real people. If I never put myself in the public eye, I will never be attacked or shamed. I have felt a lot of humiliation and shame in my life. I'd do anything to avoid it—even attack and shame myself! Kind of a funny strategy, huh?

So we've identified the unhealthy pattern and belief system: the author attacks and shames herself to keep from being attacked and shamed by other people. If you were to play a counseling role as my listening partner, how many ways could you think of to help me come back into balance? This is my list:

1. Smile warmly at the author with a loving but amused look. Ask with a gentle grin and a slightly amused tone of voice if this was a strategy she wanted to keep and what her life would be like without it. Amusement balances the tendency to take life too seriously. We give our patterns too much power when we see them as demons instead of silly costumes that we put on and forget to take off. (Please note: Helpful amusement is gentle and loving; take the same behavior too far and it becomes ridicule, which is never a useful response.)

2. Ask the author where her need to avoid harsh criticism originated: "Have you ever been attacked before?" The reason this question can provide a balance is that it draws my attention to the fact that there is nothing in the present moment that is making me behave so strangely. (I'm writing alone and nobody has read a single word yet.) The feelings feel real in the present—that's what creates the illusion—but they come from my past.

3. Ask the author to write a glowing review for herself and read it out loud. (I actually did this. It was great!)

4. Ask the author to thank her inner critics for trying to take care of her so well and ask herself if there is some other way of addressing their concerns. (I tried this, too. My first

thought was to look directly at my fear of attack.) This contradicts the author's belief that her inner critics are vicious and, therefore, bad. All defenses serve a purpose that seemed beneficial at one time.

5. Suggest to the author that she look directly at the fear by exaggerating it—to cower and protect her head with her arms and say, "Please, don't hit me!" (I meant to write "attack" here, but it came out "hit." That brought up an unpleasant memory and some tears. It's becoming clear to me now where this behavior came from, and I'm starting to feel angry.) Exaggerating the behavior reverses the pattern of trying to avoid the feelings.

6. I'd say to the author, "Good! Fight back! What do you want to say to the person who hit you?" ("How DARE you do that to me!") The counselor is encouraging the author to continue expressing the anger she reported.

7. I'd have the author push against my hands while continuing to yell, "How DARE you! (The phrase spontaneously changed to "I'm not going to let you stop me!" More tears. Then a feeling of relief and a desire to get back to work.)

Whoops! This isn't a list. It's a description of a full-fledged listening session!

All good listening sessions can produce results similar to the ones I experienced in the above example: I was able to notice that I was in the grips of an old habit and successfully freed myself from the accompanying feelings. During the next few days I wrote twice as much as I did during a similar period before the session. The habit and the feelings did come back, but when they did I was able to recognize them as my old pattern fairly quickly. Just having increased awareness of the problem was enough to enable me to get back on a more positive track. I spent no more than fifteen minutes doing the emotional work described above. Several techniques were suggested, which we'll explore in more detail in this chapter.

WAYS TO CREATE BALANCE

Creating balance can be as simple as putting on a sweater when we are too cold or taking it off when we are too warm. Creating emotional balance relies on the same concept—do more of what we do too little, and less of what we do too much—but it can be more challenging because the causes of emotional upset are often hidden or complex. Even so, there are some easy and effective approaches. The key to using these approaches is to pay attention to what is actually going on for the person you are listening to and choosing accordingly. For example, one day your friend might come to a listening session fully aware of what's going well in his or her life and ready to clean up an old hurt that is in the way of things going even better. Another day this same friend might be so lost in the pain and confusion left by that past experience that he or she can't see outside of it. You need to use a very different approach in these two situations even though the issues being worked on are the same.

Uh-oh. I can sense the anxiety levels rising now. How will you know what approach to use? Experiment! What if you make a mistake? There's no such thing as a mistake. Unlike professional psychotherapy where a client can be hurt by trusting an incompetent or unscrupulous practitioner, there is less or no expectation that the person in the counseling role in a reciprocal listening session knows more than the recipient of that attention. The expectation is that both people take responsibility for trying things out together. In fact, so-called mistakes are very important in this process. I've heard it said that God shows up in the space we leave when we stop trying to control things so tightly, when we stop trying too hard to be perfect, when we stop trying to BE God—that's when the voice of the spirit can actually be heard. This is especially true in peer counseling. When something you try doesn't work, something wonderful happens—you learn something about your partner you never would have learned otherwise. You get new information that might lead to a breakthrough for that person somewhere down the line. Use each listening session as an opportunity to learn more about each other.

None of the approaches mentioned in this book are detrimental, even when done badly. The worst that might happen is you could be left with more feelings stirred up than you successfully released. Good antidotes for this are aerobic exercise, meditation, working on a project that engages your attention fully, journal writing, or another listening session.

The Role of the Counselor

First of all, remember that when you are playing a counseling role, YOU are the most important balance of all—

- your calm, loving, nonjudgmental, clear, in-the-present attention
- your physical presence, which consists of arms to rest in, shoulders to cry on, a body to hold on to, and hands to hold
- your hopefulness, confidence, and conviction
- your patience and lack of urgency
- your ability to see and describe the truly precious qualities of your friend and the gift of being alive, and your persistence in remembering and holding out this picture for him or her, no matter what
- your commitment and refusal to give up on your friend or leave him or her alone emotionally during the course of the time you have set aside

Ninety percent of a listening session should be spent just listening and being present in the ways listed above. But if you want to provide a more specific kind of support, use your creativity to counteract the negative messages your friend carries. The following suggestions are good places to start. Because they all require the active participation of the person receiving attention, they tend to be empowering strategies that he or she can build on outside of the session. The most important strategy is self-love and appreciation.

Loving Ourselves

We expect love and appreciation to come to us through other people, but it is especially powerful and important to be able to offer this attention to ourselves. We can be with ourselves in the way we encourage a baby to begin walking—having complete confidence in her eventual success and applauding every effort towards her goal, but also being there with hugs and kisses and kind words when she falls. We're all deserving of this level of love and support no matter how old we are and what our developmental tasks are at this stage of our lives. In some respects, we never stop learning how to walk.

Loving ourselves means appreciating ourselves for who we are, not just for what we do—noticing and appreciating our goodness, intelligence, creativity, and loving, loveable nature. It means caring for ourselves and our adult needs as well as we would care for our most precious child—through creating a balance of rest, play, creativity, meaningful work, exercise, good food, connection with others and the environment, learning, thinking, and the full expression of ourselves in the world in whatever way is right for us at any given time. It means giving up any behavior that is hurtful to ourselves and those we love, especially any and all addictions. It means looking at our lives honestly and making a clear assessment of what is not going well and deciding to change it without excessive self-criticism. We've always done the best we could, given our level of awareness, information, positive experience, and emotional, physical, and spiritual resources at any given time.

This may be a great theory, but embracing these ideals and putting them into action is not always so simple. How many New Year's resolutions have we all made and broken over the years? I don't like to think about it. Thinking positively and increasing self-esteem are goals we have been encouraged to adopt for at least 40 years now, and self-help books touting the power of positive thinking continue to jump off the shelves. A particularly popular approach is the use of affirmations, positive statements used to counteract negative messages we habitually repeat to ourselves. We all have heard that these techniques work wonders but, personally, I struggle with self-love, especially affirmations. Every time I tell myself how beautiful I am, an inner voice points out all my faults. When I tell myself I am intelligent and creative I immediately think of stupid things I have done or said. When I attempt to create a daily meditation practice in which to do my affirmations, feelings of impatience, hopelessness, and boredom get in my way. I wind up frustrated and feeling bad because I can't do affirmations "right." Given my experience, you might think that I'm against the use of this technique, but that's not correct. I think affirmations are very valuable, but the way they are usually used leaves out a very significant piece of the work: releasing the feelings associated with the negative messages one is attempting to overcome.

When one successfully crafts an affirmation, the associated feelings will present themselves to be released—that's why I feel hopeless when I try certain ones. The hopelessness comes from years of unsuccessfully battling the problem the affirmation addresses. People who teach the use of affirmations always recommend creating ones that your mind can accept—ones that seem doable or potentially true. In the method I recommend, this is not necessary. Use the affirmation that most directly opposes the negative programming you wish to overcome, then bring it to a focused listening session.

Using Affirmations as a Counseling Technique

When you are receiving attention, create a simple affirmation with your partner that contradicts a negative message you carry. One I was given recently is "My life is a beautiful expression of the Divinity within all things." Say the affirmation out loud—not like a mantra or chant, but as a statement of fact. Say it with feeling. Exaggerate it. Use a completely positive tone of voice, facial expression, and body posture. Stand up, put your head up, throw your arms open wide, and shout the affirmation from the rooftops! It's difficult to use affirmations this way without feeling some emotion—and that's exactly the purpose of this approach. Allow the feelings to be expressed and relate any memories that come up, then go back and do the affirmation again until it feels true or a new, more appropriate affirmation comes to mind. Your listening partner's job is to encourage you and cheer you on.

If you feel so much resistance to this approach that it's not useful, there are several other ways to work with affirmations. The most useful one is for the person playing the counseling role to model the affirmation for you. Many people have so much performance anxiety that it is easier to feel their feelings while watching somebody else express the affirmation crafted on their behalf. The counselor could also simply appreciate you straight forwardly; however, the benefit of trying on different ways of saying an affirmation, especially the more outrageous ones, is that it interrupts habitual physical patterns that stop you from feeling. Because these physical patterns stem from habits of the mind, it seems to work equally well to just imagine yourself doing the affirmation in a completely exultant fashion while watching someone else model it.

Another approach is to try saying the affirmation out loud a few times any way you can. Then have your partner feed you the following statement: "If this statement were true, it would mean _____. What's your first thought?" Answer this question several times.

You could also try closing your eyes and imagining yourself as a little baby. Pretend to be the baby's parent—the most loving parent that child could ever want. Hold the baby in your arms, and tell her or him the affirmation, in this case "Your life is a beautiful expression of the Divinity within all things." Does it sound true for the child? Then it must be true for you. Let that message sink in. It's so easy to see the preciousness of a baby, and so difficult to believe it about ourselves. Yet, deep inside, despite all the hurts we carry and the negative patterns of behavior we have learned, we are the same precious beings we were when we were born. Let any feelings well up and flow.

At the end of the session set a few mini-goals that will lead toward implementing the affirmation in your life. For example, if I believed the affirmation I've been working with is true, I would never again put myself down for making mistakes. I would see mistakes as a necessary step in my evolution and celebrate them. A goal I could set might be to make a note about what I learn from any mistakes or to notice that despite my failings, things generally work out anyway. I could decide to tell my listening partner mistakes I made and celebrate them. Or I could decide to simply forgive myself and remind myself that I get to be "perfectly human."

In your next listening session, report back to your partner about how implementing these goals went.

Self-Forgiveness and Thanks

Self-forgiveness is invaluable in changing negative habits and messages into positive ones. I often fail to measure up to the standards I have accepted or set for myself. No matter how true an affirmation about my intelligence might be, the fact remains that I *do* say things that I or others judge as stupid. No matter how loving I may be at my core, I still do things that hurt other people sometimes. Reciting affirmations at times like these just makes me feel miserable because every ounce of my being is screaming, "It's a lie!"

A counselor once asked me, "Can you forgive yourself, Sheryl? Can you forgive yourself for being human?" It was very powerful, perhaps one of the most powerful counseling experiences I have had. Like me, you will not always succeed at implementing your affirmations and goals. You didn't walk very well for the first few years of your life either. You get to fall down. You get to make mistakes. Give yourself permission to do so and forgive yourself for your failings, always.

I have also found that appreciating myself for taking a step toward a change I've been working on works extremely well. For example, I decided to improve my eating habits but needed to spend more time preparing my meals to do so. Following through on this intention felt like hard work. Then one evening, during the moment of silence my husband and I observe before meals, I spontaneously thanked myself for making such a great dinner. My mood instantly improved! It was also easier to cook the next night. Make it a habit to appreciate yourself for any successes, no matter how small. A little positive reinforcement goes a long way. Starting every listening session by relating any successes you've had since your last meeting creates a habit of self-reinforcement and adds the positive benefits of allowing your partner to cheer you on and celebrate with you.

self-appreciation meditation

Allow 10–15 minutes for this meditation.

Sit comfortably in a chair or lie on your back and place one of your hands over your heart and the other over your belly. Breathe deeply and feel the warmth of your hands on your body. Imagine that there is healing energy in your hands that is nurturing you and filling you with love. As you receive this positive attention, acknowledge aspects of yourself that you appreciate—your strengths and positive qualities, the big and small ways you have helped yourself, other people, or the world, the times that you tried even if you didn't succeed. Remember the people you have touched and the people who have touched you. Breathe deeply and allow any feelings that arise to flow.

Loving Others

Some people say that the ability to love others is more important than being loved by others. It is definitely a measure of one's self-esteem and mental health. In national surveys people who volunteer regularly report that their health and sense of well-being improves the more they volunteer and the more personal contact they have with the people they are helping. There are also indications from other studies that helping others strengthens the immune system, decreases pain, and helps eliminate attitudes of hostility.

The value of loving others is what every religion and spiritual agency has professed throughout the ages. Some spiritual teachers even recommend sending light or love through meditative practices to unhappy people, world leaders, and troubled places around the world. In my listening partnerships I have learned how valuable this can be. In many respects being in the counseling role is just as valuable for one's mental health as being in the receiver's role, perhaps more so.

Sometimes I can't figure out what to do to help one of my friends—they've dug themselves a hole they can't see out of, and I can't figure out how to help them, no matter how hard I try. At times like this I fall back on the most basic of all attentive listening skills: I stop talking and consciously allow love to fill my heart and beam out to my friend. Within a few minutes he or she will suddenly notice me. People actually appear startled for a second and then something shifts. On many occasions I have seen people burst into tears; other times they laugh embarrassedly and try to go back to rehearsing their hopeless, powerless stance to find that they can't find the words or that they can't believe it anymore. I'm always amazed because I haven't said or done anything other than smile at them with love and delight. Intellectually, I don't understand how something so simple could have such a dramatic effect, but I've seen it happen so many times that I don't even question its value anymore.

But even more amazing than the effect it has on my partner is the effect it has on me. As a counselor I get dramatic proof that just my aware, loving presence can make a difference to another human being. That shoots my feelings of self-esteem sky-high, and I leave those sessions feeling empowered to do anything else I choose for the rest of the day. I also feel more inspired to continue helping people, not only through counseling, but also through sharing my skills and attention in other ways.

It is not always easy to show our love and delight openly. We don't normally give each other permission to do this outside the context of romantic relationships or parent-child dynamics. In fact, when someone breaks the "rules" it is very common for people to confuse such attention with a romantic come-on or to unconsciously start treating the person like a parent or guru. Professional psychotherapists run into this problem all the time. They call it "transference." Transference is a common type of projection, a concept I'll go into in more detail in Chapter 6.

Another problem many of us have with showing love is that we have been taught that loving means merging with another person. We try to see the world through our loved ones' eyes to such an extent that we lose our balance and sense of self. Mutual experiences of oneness with a loved one can be ecstatic, but everyday practical loving involves unconditional, positive regard and being commited to each other's growth while staying aware of our own thoughts, feelings, and physicalness. We'll explore this more fully in the next chapter.

For now, if you find it difficult to allow yourself to love openly, take a look at some of your past experiences. Has anyone ever developed a crush on you that got in the way of having a mutually acceptable relationship? Have you ever done that with someone else? Have you ever been rejected or abused by someone you loved? We all hold a lot of humiliation, hurt, and disappointment that make us hide our hearts away. Talk about these experiences in a listening session and make an agreement with your partner that, at least in the context of these sessions, you will give each other permission to be close. When you have worked through enough of your pain, use your listening sessions to forgive people who have hurt you as a way of bringing the healing to completion.

Additionally, it will be helpful to your relationship and to your life if all your needs for sharing and receiving love are not relegated to this one relationship. This is especially important if your listening partner is your spouse or lover. If issues come up between you, you'll need other people who can think clearly about you and your relationship. Having listening partnerships with more than one person is a very good idea. We all have different blindspots and places of clarity. Make a commitment to help each other develop as many close friendships and diverse community connections as you want.

buddhist loving kindness meditation

Allow 15–20 minutes for this meditation.

Sit comfortably in a chair or on a meditation cushion. Breathe and let your body relax. Let go of the cares of the day and feel your breath as you inhale and exhale. Imagine that as you inhale you breathe in love and as you exhale you release love out into the environment around you. Then silently recite the following phrases.

> "May I be filled with loving kindness.
> May I be happy.
> May I be well.
> May I be peaceful.
> May I be free."

You might want to picture yourself as a young child or simply feel your body as it is today. Feel your heart open and let the feelings flow through. Keep repeating the phrases for several minutes, adjusting the wording if necessary.

When you feel ready, think of someone who has cared for you, someone you love or feel grateful toward. Picture that person in your mind and repeat the same phrases, changing the word "I" to "he" or "she." Imagine that you breathe in love and send that love to your friend on the exhale. Continue for several minutes.

If you would like, repeat this meditation with other friends, family members, teachers, groups of people, people everywhere, animals, the earth, or the universe. You could even try picturing a difficult person, someone you don't get along with or feel kindly toward. Consider adding the phrase "I forgive you."

What's Going Well?

A student in one of my classes told me that a key part of his healing from alcohol addiction was learning to notice the beauty of every moment. Earlier I recommended starting every attentive listening session by remembering what's been good since the last meeting. Often my students can't think of anything the first time I ask them to do this. I always say that, despite their feelings, if they listed every good thing about their lives, it would be a much longer list than their list of problems and complaints. Was the sun shining today? Did you hear a bird sing? Did you have breakfast? Do you have a roof over your head? Not everyone can say yes to all of these things. It is important to notice the blessings you have. If you notice everything that is great about being alive every day, you will feel happy to be alive. If you notice what is good about your life, you will have a good life! But don't trust me on this—try it for yourself. Pick a time every day when you will remember what was good about the day. Before the evening meal works well for anyone who was brought up with the concept of saying grace. My husband and I tell each other the "highlights" of our day every night before going to sleep so that our last thoughts before drifting off are pleasant ones.

The reason we do this at the beginning of listening sessions is because so much of our attention is habitually consumed by worries and problems. By breaking that pattern right at the start of a session we allow ourselves to shift into a broader and more balanced perspective for looking at our lives. It is much easier to take a powerful proactive approach to making improvements from this vantage point.

Now I walk in beauty
Beauty is before me
Beauty is behind me
Above and below me

HOPI CHANT

What's Been Hard?

We all need a place to vent our frustrations and complaints. During much of the time we spend with other people we need to adopt a "put on a happy face" attitude. When you have a deadline to meet, your boss doesn't want to hear about your sick child keeping you awake all night. Your neighbor will feel uncomfortable if you complain about your sexual problems. Your mother might worry excessively if you tell her your financial concerns. Your children will be frightened if you dump your fears in their laps. There are so many times when we need to be "brave little soldiers," it's a great relief when we get an opportunity to let go and be authentic about our lives.

When you are playing a counseling role, allow your friend to tell you how hard it's been without interrupting or trying to fix things by giving advice or jumping in too quickly with a suggestion designed to balance the pain. Truly being heard in a respectful way is often the very balance we need. Trust that your friend will work out his or her own difficulties, that when cloudy emotions are cleared, new creative solutions and perspectives will appear.

If something upsetting has recently happened to your friend, encourage him to tell you the whole story. If you notice that he is holding back emotion at any point (look for a tightened jaw or mouth, a wrinkled brow, clenched fists, a slight quiver in the voice, or a catch in the throat), gently remind him that it is okay to feel whatever he is feeling. Have him repeat parts of the story that seem to have an emotional charge ("Could you tell me that part again?"). If he is telling the story very quickly (a common way of avoiding feelings), remind him that you have plenty of time and you are very interested in what he has to say. Ask him to take his time. Don't worry if there is no dramatic emotional discharge such as tears or trembling. Just telling the story can release emotional tension.

What Does That Remind You Of?

Sometimes an upsetting event occurs and our emotional reaction is totally out of proportion to what happened. This is an especially noticeable phenomena with small children—a two-year-old can throw a full-scale tantrum because her brother has the blue cup and she has to use the red one. But adults do this, too. A co-worker can unintentionally say something that throws our whole day into disarray as we fret about the meaning behind the remark and our reactions to it. Usually, the experience is symbolic of a greater internal dynamic or it reminds us of an earlier incident that we have not dealt with fully.

By asking your listening partner, "Does this incident remind you of anything that's ever happened to you before?" you allow him or her to separate reactivated feelings left over from past experiences from the reality of the present moment. This is even more powerful if you call attention to how the present moment is better than how it was before or if you can *create* a present moment that is better. For example, in the sample session at the beginning of this chapter, I eventually identified the pattern of self-criticism as coming from abuse I experienced as a child. At that age I could never have safely stood up to my oppressors, so to release the feelings in the session, I said what I would have liked to have said in the past, and I fought back without doing any real harm by physically pushing against my counselor's hands.

It is also important to work on the earliest related memory you have, if you can. Our brain stores information about similar incidents in such a way that the memories of these incidents are connected to each other in a chain. When you relate one incident, an earlier incident will often come to mind. If you work on the earliest memory, feelings left from later experiences of a similar nature will be released at the same time.

Many people find it important to tell the stories of what happened many times. Other people, like myself, find it overwhelming to look directly at these early memories. It is not necessary to focus on the old stories; the important thing is to counteract the hurtful experience by bringing attention to present-day resources and abilities you didn't have in the past. We're literally changing the ending to the stories (myths) we've been living by.

Rewriting Our Life Stories

My maternal grandparents were born in a little village near Odessa, Russia, at the turn of the century. The story of "Fiddler on the Roof" in many ways is their story— poor people living a traditional Jewish life being forced to leave their community and resettle in a strange land after suffering many losses and being separated from their loved ones. I once heard a story about how when the first Jews from Russia came to the United States they were in great despair and found it hard to support each other emotionally because they each desperately needed to be supported themselves. They found themselves questioning the existence of God. How could God have let such terrible things happen? The spiritual focus of the community was crumbling, and that threatened the community's survival as a whole.

One day the rabbi of one of these communities told his tiny congregation a story that changed their outlook and refocused their energies in a positive way. He said that when they were dead they would be given the opportunity to hang their sorrows on the Tree of Life and trade them for the sorrows of anyone else they chose. The dead would walk around the tree, and as they walked they would be seeing with illuminated eyes all the patterns of the world, the past, present, and future, and the meaning of every event that took place in the universe. They would see how their individual sorrows had led to the blessings they experienced later in life or how the experiences had taught them lessons they needed to learn to help other people. They would see how their fate as a community affected other communities, how it inspired people who would not otherwise have been inspired to take positive action, how it taught the world valuable lessons and brought it to a better place. In the end, when it came time to choose, each person would choose their own sorrows.

When I first moved to Santa Cruz years ago, I heard a radio psycho-spiritual counselor suggest to a caller who grew up with sexual abuse that she chose her parents and life lessons before she was born. I was shocked and angry. How could anyone suggest that a person would choose such a thing? I wanted nothing to do with a belief system that I believed blamed the victim for present-day difficulties.

Then one day I suddenly had the idea that, as ridiculous as it might be to believe that I chose my childhood circumstances, it might be useful to tell my life story from that perspective anyway. What if it were true? What if I chose to do some particular work in this lifetime and chose the life I was born into to teach me what I needed to learn to fulfill that destiny? How would I describe my childhood then? I tried it out and suddenly saw the events of my life fall into a recognizable and meaningful pattern. Events that previously looked horrific now could be seen as powerful catalysts; people I hated for their cruelty looked forgivable; every terrible experience could be seen as the seed for every delicious fruit I've eaten since. That's when I remembered the Tree of Life story I have told above. I realized that to some extent I was looking at my life with the eyes of someone walking around the Tree of Life, and I saw that the rabbi's story was true. I wouldn't trade my life for anyone else's.

Retelling one's life story from a positive perspective expands on the idea that we live our lives according to the myths we tell ourselves about who we are, how we came to be that way, and what we are capable of being as a result. It can be very challenging to do this particular exercise—we all tend to be very attached to our feelings of victimhood, so it can be hard to notice the positive benefits we or the world gained from our hurtful experiences. If you persist, however, it may be enlightening. I discovered I now had reasons to feel proud of myself in the very same areas I felt ashamed in my childhood. Those terrible experiences had spurred me on to moments of greatness. You could rewrite your life story privately by working in a journal, but if you tell your story out loud in a listening session or elsewhere, it will have a much more powerful impact.

If the spiritual approach doesn't appeal to you, there are many other ways to work with your life story. Choose one pattern of behavior or limiting belief. After tracking down its origins in your history, tell your story about it, making sure to include the new limitless behaviors and beliefs that you are capable of today. For example, here's how I might tell the story of why I criticize myself so much:

"Once upon a time there was a shy and sensitive little girl who was eager to make friends but was unsure of how to do it. She was brought up in a culture and family system that was very different from her classmates, so the behaviors that were acceptable—even required of her—in her family were almost completely foreign to everyone else around her. She was scapegoated by her peers, constantly ridiculed, and physically harassed everyday on the playground and between classes. She ate her lunches alone and played by herself at recess and after school. This continued for several years until Sheryl was so convinced that she deserved this behavior that she learned how to fit in by turning against herself. She learned how to laugh at jokes made at her expense and how to behave like the "good Irish Catholic child" she wasn't. She changed her own behavior by anticipating ahead of time criticism she might receive and making the changes she hoped would keep that criticism from happening. By the time she was an adult, this behavior was so ingrained she couldn't remember being any other way.

But, luckily, as an adult she developed friends who respected her and encouraged her growth. She learned new skills and created a more diverse community for herself. She even traveled across the country to a place where a wide variety of behaviors are acceptable and even celebrated. And now she knows that—despite any feelings to the contrary—she never deserved to be attacked. She is good and kind and completely lovable exactly the way she is…and she always was."

Telling this story makes me cry. If I were in a counseling role listening to someone else tell a similar tale, it would touch me deeply. Without my training as a peer counselor it might even be difficult for me to listen effectively because of my own reactivated childhood pain. In the next chapter we'll explore ways of staying effective in the listening role in situations where we might over-identify with someone else's story.

Raincoats and Sunbonnets

"You cannot stop the birds of sadness from flying over your head,
but you can prevent them from nesting in your hair."

PYGMY PROVERB

In Western society one of the biggest pitfalls on the path of true intimacy is to lose oneself in someone else's experience. We all do this at one time or another—find ourselves worrying about our friends when they are not in our presence, feeling like crying when someone else is crying, being unable to separate out our own thoughts and feelings in the presence of strong emotions, and carrying around the thoughts and feelings others express as if they were our own. While the techniques in this chapter will not make you immune to other people's feelings (I'm not sure that's even desirable), they will help you remain sufficiently centered so that you will be able to provide assistance without becoming overwhelmed or taking the pain on as your own.

EMOTIONAL SENSITIVITY AND CHILDHOOD CONDITIONING

Researchers have shown that infants respond to the emotions of their mothers from the earliest age they've been able to test, yet as adults we show a very wide variation in our willingness to notice and respond to other people's emotions. Why?

One theory is based on the fact that when you are faced with conflicting information from your senses, you either integrate the conflicting information or selectively attend to what seems to be most important and disregard the rest. A young child might hear his mother talking sweetly and calmly but sense from her tight face that she is angry. In some cultures responding to the mother's emotion might be considered a good thing. But the majority of people in the United States expect that when they hide their emotions, the pretense is to be respected. Direct responses to emotions a person is trying to hide or deny usually leads to embarassment or anger.

Children brought up in these conditions learn very early to habitually disregard emotion they would otherwise perceive. They don't respond to "hidden emotions" because they learn not to see them. In an abusive or alcoholic family, the consequences of ignoring emotions can be worse than seeing them. If Dad gets violent when he's drunk or gets drunk when he's unhappy or stressed, it is very important to family members to codependently detect underlying emotions and respond to them before the situation gets out of hand. A child in this situation will tend to disregard the calm veneer and stay aware of the feelings. In the previous example, where shutting down awareness becomes an habitual response, this focusing of awareness may also become a rigid pattern instead of a decision.

Ideally, we want to be able to use our attention like a camera lens—zooming in when we want a close-up, switching to a wide angle when we want the big picture, and moving smoothly back and forth in the midrange according to the needs of the moment. Some people have their cameras set to such a narrow field of vision that the person they focus on fills the viewfinder. Their own concerns are left behind as life revolves around the feelings and behaviors of another person. People who learned the opposite pattern of ignoring emotion may find it easier to remain detached but often struggle in relationships at home and at work because of their learned insensitivity. Some people bounce back and forth between these extremes. The information in this chapter isn't necessary for many people, but if you find yourself getting swamped by your partner's feelings, the techniques here will help you to explore ways to use sensitivity in a healthy way.

SHIFTING ONE'S ATTENTION

Tibetan Buddhist monks are famous for being able to listen with both compassion and detachment. It is very powerful to be held in the loving gaze of such a person, knowing that no matter how badly one feels he will not waver in his ability to pay attention. The power of love and the stability of detachment provide the balance we need to be effective counselors in all situations. Unfortunately, very few of us have the necessary life experience to listen in such a way without a great deal of practice. Learning to shift attention in and out at will helps develop both detachment and sensitivity.

In listening sessions we have a perfect opportunity to experiment with shifting our attention because the mechanics of the session require it. We always start by getting centered physically by breathing deeply from our bellies and paying attention to our breath for a few brief moments. This is a time-honored method for pulling attention away from distressing emotions and thoughts. When we take on the role of counselor, our job involves providing a stable loving presence for our friends so they can safely have part of their attention in the present moment and part on the old distress they are trying to release without worrying about upsetting us. Eventually you may learn to split your attention between your breath and your love for them. For now it is enough to remember to relax and breath at all.

The second step in a listening session is to allow the other person to fill our sphere of attention and purposely decide to shift our own thoughts, feelings, and reactions into the background to get a clear impression of their thoughts, feelings, and world-view. The difference between this and certain types of codependent behavior is that in a listening session we use this skill conciously. Narrowing our focus of attention *intentionally* helps us retain the ability to intentionally shift it back out when needed.

In a session we need to focus enough to gain accurate information about our friend, but we also need to avoid identifying so strongly with the person that we become submerged in their feelings and thoughts and lose our ability to be of service to them. The task of identifying a person's patterns and negative belief systems and then crafting ways to create emotional balance prods us to shift our attention back out and helps prevent us from getting stuck in an overly identified state.

If, as counselor, you sense that you have lost yourself in your partner's pain or confusion, or that you are likely to, shift your attention partially to noticing how your body feels in the present moment. It helps to literally shift your body weight. Take a deep breath as you do so and break eye contact for a second or two. If you need to, intensify awareness of your body by breathing into your belly and letting your weight sink into your chair or into the floor.

If noticing your body isn't enough to break your identification with your partner's story, shift your perspective further back. What would your friend's problem look like from the vantage point of 25 years from now? With enough distance, I can always remember that most of the time whatever is going on is just an insignificant blip on the screen of life. In fact, once my partner is free of this position, the thoughts and feelings she is so caught up in will be insignificant to her as well. This reminds me not to take it so seriously. Then I shift my attention close in again, but now I can hold an attitude of loving amusement. ("I love you, but you're operating under a creative illusion—you don't need to be limited by that anymore.")

You can practice similar skills outside of a listening session by trying the following exercises.

groundedness—a guided meditation

Being grounded means having your attention in the present moment, alert, aware of emotions but not thrown off by them. The purpose of this exercise is to give yourself a bodily sense of calm, groundedness, and determination.

Stand with your feet slightly apart and knees slightly bent. Close your eyes, or allow your gaze to become soft and unfocused. Relax and slow down your breathing, putting particular attention on a slower exhalation. Continue this for several breaths.

Now let your abdomen relax, dropping your shoulders and letting your chest open, more and more as you breathe. Feel your belly rise and fall with each inhalation and exhalation. Keep doing this for a few minutes until you feel relaxed.

Become aware of the soles of your feet...feel each point of contact your feet make with the ground—the balls of your feet, the heel, each toe...imagine that your feet are so heavy that they actually sink into the surface you're standing on, as if you were at the beach with your feet submerged in the sand...imagine yourself growing roots down into the earth from the soles of your feet...send those roots deep down into the earth all the way to the earth's core...imagine these roots drawing strength from the earth and let that sense of strength travel slowly up your roots, through your feet and legs and right up your spine to the top of your head.

Now think of all the people who support you in your life as well as any aspect of the universe that you know supports you at this time. Feel the presence of all these supporters standing firmly behind you, supporting you with their hands, their strength, and their love. Breathe in that support and let it mix with the energy you are drawing from the earth.

Feel the strength and firmness of your body supported by the earth. Know that you can return to this feeling of support at any time simply by remembering it.

Take some final deep breaths...open your eyes and keep this grounded feeling with you. Now you are ready to face whatever comes your way from a place of calm, strength, and support.

shifting awareness meditation

Start this meditation in the usual fashion. Sit comfortably on a chair or meditation cushion, close your eyes gently, and breathe deeply once or twice all the way down to your belly. Feel your belly rise and fall with each inhalation and exhalation. Allow extraneous thoughts and worries to drop away and, without trying to control it, simply pay attention to your breath as it moves in your body. Notice where you feel it—in your belly, your chest, your upper back, your throat, or at your nostrils. Do you feel any other sensations? Allow your attention to move from one part of your body to the next, noticing how each part feels without changing anything.

When you are ready, allow your attention to shift to external sounds. What do you hear in the environment around you? Allow your attention to shift from sounds that are close by to ones that are softer and far away. Then focus on the closer ones again. Finally, shift your awareness to internal sounds. Can you hear your heart beat or the sound of your own breathing? Return again and notice your breath and how it feels as it moves in your body. Has anything changed? Now shift back to listening. Can you listen to external sounds and feel your breath at the same time?

Return to simply breathing and then gently open your eyes. Allow your gaze to fall on the floor a few feet in front of you. Continue to breathe and focus on the floor. Is it carpeted, wood, or linoleum? Or, if you are outside, grass, dirt, rock, etc.? Notice the texture and color, the light reflected in it, or shadows. Are you still breathing? Can you feel your breath and focus visually at the same time? Move your eyes slightly and broaden your field of vision. Take in a more panaramic view and continue to breathe. As you gaze out, listen to external sounds as well. Add awareness of smell. And continue to feel the physical sensations of your own body.

When you are ready to finish, close your eyes and take several deep breaths, then open your eyes and stretch.

attention in the head, heart, and hara

In the martial arts, people learn to focus their attention in their hara (in the belly, just below the navel) in order to stay grounded and safe. This exercise demonstrates the difference such attention can make. You will need to practice with another person.

1. Walk about the room in your normal fashion. Now purposely focus attention in your head and continue walking about. (For many people this is their normal fashion.) Notice what that is like, how visually oriented you are in this state, what your energy feels like, how heavy or light you feel. Do you feel safe?

2. Walk about now with your attention in your heart, as if you have eyes in your chest. Notice how that feels and if it is different from focusing in your head. Many people feel more connected to other people in this state.

3. Now walk with your attention in your hara. Feel your breath centered in your belly and as you walk allow the movement to come from there. How does that feel? Many people become aware of having feet for the first time during this exercise. Often people report feeling heavier or more solid.

4. Now you and your partner will work standing still. Experiment with putting your attention alternately in your head, heart, and hara while your partner lightly pushes against your chest with one hand. Do this without making eye contact with him or her. Most people find that when their attention is in their head, they lose their balance when their partner pushes them. When their attention is in their hara, their partner cannot push them over without using extra force.

(continued)

attention in the head, heart, and hara (continued)

5. Switch roles so both people can experience this phenomena.

6. Now experiment with making eye contact. Without training, most people find it difficult to make eye contact and stay grounded. Experiment with putting your attention in your hara while your partner lightly pushes against your chest without eye contact and then keeping it there as your eyes meet. Most people need to practice this, but it is a skill well worth learning.

OTHER WAYS TO MAINTAIN ONE'S BALANCE AROUND OTHER PEOPLE'S PAIN

1. Avoid unconsciously being a mirror for other people. Many healing modalities encourage the healer or counselor to mirror their client—to match the client's energy, breathing, tone of voice, facial expressions, etc.—to establish rapport and an empathic connection. Some particularly sensitive people do this same thing as one of their natural habits. However, if you match other people for too long without being very intentional about it, especially in emotionally rich situations such as a listening session, this is the most surefire way to lose yourself and your ability to think in a flexible manner. In a session your partner may be caught in the illusion of unreleased pain. It's not healthy to match that pain and confusion for very long. Instead, once you have a sense of what the problem is, take a moment to shift your perspective and adopt a physical posture that will counteract the unbalanced state your partner is in. In other words, in addition to suggesting an affirmation or action for them to do, act out the posture and tone of voice that will be the most beneficial.

For example, if your friend is fearful or shy, you might offer an affirmation celebrating his or her ability to be relaxed and confident while acting so relaxed that you flop over or so confident that you could be mistaken for a comic book superhero. When you are actively working to combat the effects of negative feelings, you will no longer be caught up in them yourself.

2. Sometimes people are *too* active and vocal in the counseling role because their discomfort with other people's emotion pushes them to try too hard to fix things. The most powerful emotional assistance that exists—purposely sending love to the person you are listening to—requires no external effort or talking. Some people imagine being filled with love from a divine source and sending the excess out. Drop all expectation of directing this healing energy and trust that it will go where it is needed without you directing it to be used for a specific purpose. Be confident that your friend will make good use of your attention in whatever way is appropriate for him or her, provided enough safety has been established. Not trying to fix things combined with the love in your face will help that person feel you have confidence in him or her and help create the safety needed.

3. If you have no trouble listening to a variety of problems but lose your perspective around certain topics or expressions of emotion, you have received a strong clue that some issue from your own past has been triggered. If you get sessions on those issues yourself, they will noticeably help you maintain your balance in a relatively short period of time.

4. If you chronically find it difficult to be around emotional expression, you may have had earlier experiences where your own feelings were squelched or where other people used their emotion as an excuse to abuse you. Learning to set healthy boundaries (see the next section)

and reclaiming the parts of yourself you were forced to give up will help you feel more relaxed and confident.

5. When all else fails, I stop the session and ask for five minutes for myself. It's embarrassing for me to do this, but being totally overwhelmed and ineffectual is embarrassing, too. It makes a difference to be honest: it releases the tension in the situation. It also automatically shifts my perspective and gives me some distance when I have permission NOT to pay attention to someone for five minutes. Your partner will appreciate your renewed attention when you focus on him or her more fully.

BOUNDARY SETTING

Boundaries are the border between where you and your needs and desires leave off and where other people and their needs and desires begin. All parents inadvertently and sometimes purposely disregard a child's needs and desires. Abusive parents, however, rip holes in those boundaries by forcing the child to make paying attention to the adult a higher priority than focusing on the child's own concerns. The rights to control what happens to one's body, to feel one's own feelings, and think one's own thoughts, even the right to simply BE, are temporarily given up whenever a child is subjected to physical, sexual, emotional, or verbal violence. If you were forced to give up your boundaries repeatedly as a child, you probably struggle with the concept of healthy boundaries in your present-day relationships. It is hard to set limits and be aware of your own needs when your attention is excessively focused on other people.

Additionally, boundaries are often culturally based. If you grew up in a different culture, you may be confused about appropriate boundaries in this culture. For example, in California what most people consider to be friendly, platonic physical contact might be misconstrued as a sexual come-on in New England. Conversely, a "normal" amount of emotional expression on the East Coast could be perceived as a psychic attack on the West Coast.

Learning to set boundaries that are appropriate for you and learning to respect boundaries other people set (even if they seem excessive by your standards) will go a long way toward healing earlier abuse and creating present-day relationships that are respectful, loving, and safe.

Ways to Work on Boundary Issues in a Listening Session

1. In the last chapter I recommended making the decision to be close with your listening partner. For someone with boundary issues, that might be a frightening suggestion or misconstrued as encouragement to be sexual. It is not necessary to be sexual to be close emotionally; neither is it necessary to give up any boundaries you require for safety. Explore this topic in your next listening session.

2. Experiment with physical distance in your listening session. Make eye contact with each other from across the room. Try moving closer to your partner slowly until there is a change in how you feel, note the feeling then continue moving in. For example, you might feel very uncomfortable far away, feel more comfortable at a medium distance, and then uncomfortable as you get even closer. At what points did your comfort level change? Does it make a difference if you remain still and your partner moves toward you? Experiment with setting boundaries by asking your partner to stop moving toward you or to move further away. How does that feel? If it is uncomfortable to tell your partner to move back, practice doing so in this and future sessions.

   Ideal boundaries are flexible ones that change with the circumstances and with time. Come back to this exercise later and notice if anything has changed. If not, you might want to play with pushing your edges of discomfort just a little.

3. While making eye contact say the word "no." Play with different tones of voice and facial expressions. Be silly with it—light, breezy, completely cheerful. Then try it more seriously.

   If it is hard to say "no" seriously, say it quietly at first—just a whisper—then little by little get louder until you are shouting. It is very important that you only vocalize as loudly for as long as you can maintain eye contact, and when you get loud, yell from your belly, not from your throat. Feel your power as it rises up and let the energy release. If any thoughts or memories come up, say them out loud. If you remember a situation when it would have been useful to have been able to stick up for yourself, imagine yourself back there actually doing so. Tell the story as if it happened that way. Let your partner play the role of the person you needed to stand up to, call your partner by that person's name, and say "no." If your partner can handle it, you could even push against their hands physically. He or she should offer you enough resistance so that you actually have something to push against, but the resistance should not overpower you.

   If saying "no" in an angry way comes easily but staying light is difficult, practice smiling and saying "no" cheerfully while your listening partner begs, pleads, or demands that you say "yes." Relate any memories that come up and devise role-playing that counteracts your childhood experiences as above.

4. If being aware of yourself around other people without being self-conscious is difficult, try using your sessions to pay attention to yourself relaxed in the presence of another person. Lie down, close your eyes if you like, and pay attention to how you feel physically and/or emotionally in the present moment. This may feel impossible, but with your friend's beaming approval, encouragement, and con-

fidence in your eventual success, you will eventually be successful. The listener's main job is to stand guard. He or she might quietly remind you of their presence by holding your hand or by holding you in their arms (only with your consent), but they should not suggest any affirmations, topics of conversation, or actions for you to do or expect you to talk, make eye contact, release emotion, or even stay awake. If you choose to do any of these things, of course, that is fine, but it is not necessary. The idea is that you get to be fully with yourself in the present moment in the presence of another person who is delighted with you exactly as you are just because you're alive. You don't have to pay attention to them or do anything else in order to stay safe or keep them interested in you. Several sessions like this can work wonders for anyone who was ever forced to jump through hoops for positive attention or forced to be different from who they really are to stay safe. It is an especially useful approach to use with men. Because of the way men are trained in our society, many of them find permission to just "be" the most valuable time they can spend.

5. People with hurt boundaries often carry a recording that says other people's emotions are hurtful to them or that they are responsible for other people's emotions. To work with difficulties listening to someone cry, have your listening partner pretend to cry in the most playful, exaggerated way possible. (Waaah! Waaah!) Say anything that comes to mind while they're doing that and share any memories. You could also try pretending to cry in an exaggerated way yourself and see what that brings up. Don't censor your thoughts. If memories come up about times people were abusive in their expression of emotion either to you or in your presence, retell the stories from the perspective of how it should have been for you—how you should have

been treated or how it would have been if you could have spoken up for yourself or knew you had some capability you know you have now. Play with other expressions of emotion you have trouble with in the same way. (The key word here is "play"—getting to laugh at something that usually disturbs you is the best way to gain a new perspective.)

How to Set Healthy Boundaries

Most people in our society have some confusion about healthy boundaries. Working on these issues will not only help you be a better listener but will improve your relationships in many respects. We live in a culture that says it is a virtue to put other people's needs ahead of our own; and, in fact, there are circumstances such as parenting a young child or helping out in a crisis that demand it. However, many of us embraced a message that says our own needs and desires are less important than other people's. Women, in particular, are trained to put their own concerns last. Learning to check in with yourself first before taking care of others, and making sure that you make your own health and well-being a priority, even when you are purposely in a caretaking position, is a good habit to develop.

It may be fruitful to examine the places where you automatically give away your time, energy, and resources without thinking about it. For example, it is not necessary to play a counseling role every time your listening partner or anyone else you are close to desires it. In fact, the main reason that I suggest listening sessions be special times set aside specifically for the purpose of trading emotional assistance is because many people need assistance with setting healthy boundaries in this area. People who had abusive or emotionally needy parents were sometimes forced into a counseling role as children. Additionally, women and men in this society are often expected to play counselor as a condition of their marriages, regardless of their own emotional state. Ask your loved ones to refrain from dumping their feelings on you without permission except when you have made a conscious decision to be in a listening role. You'll have a chance to get emotionally centered and they will receive better attention if you set a boundary in this area.

Conversely, some of us develop the habit of fiercely guarding against excessive involvements with others to the extent of building walls that keep us isolated or focused excessively on ourselves and our own concerns. It can be just as useful to notice where you automatically say "no" as the places where you unthinkingly say "yes."

It is very common for people with hurt boundaries to confuse making commitments to others with giving up their boundaries. Some common patterns are to fulfill commitments rigidly despite any abuse we experience in the process, to avoid commitment like the plague, never saying "yes" without great anxiety, or to choose people to interact with who don't make demands or commitments themselves so we never have to deal with the issue at all. In reality, all commitment really means is deciding what we want and putting our energy in that direction 100 percent, with persistence. Start your healing and growth in this area by making a lifelong commitment to yourself first and foremost, and then allow yourself to take some chances with making commitments in other areas (making the decision that no further commitments you make will take precedence over your health and well-being). If you work on any emotional issues that get stirred up in this process, you will eventually succeed in reclaiming commitment as a positive force in your life.

The ability to make a commitment to ourselves is the first step in learning to set healthy boundaries and stay grounded in social situations. The next step is to assume that everyone you interact with is eager to be your close, dependable ally and friend and would welcome the opportunity to learn how to do that better as long as the intention is reciprocated. Generally speaking, except in cases where a person was extremely hurt or is under the influence of drug or alcohol addiction, human beings naturally desire comfortable relationships with other people. On the other hand, we all grew up with different cultural and family patterns. What may be an obvious boundary from your viewpoint may be an arbitrary restriction on closeness from another person's perspective. Don't assume that it is someone else's responsibility to guess what your boundaries are or, once informed, to automatically remember those boundaries without being reminded.

Remembering that most people are eager to have good relationships with you will help ease a common difficulty most people have with the boundary-setting process. It can be challenging to learn to stand up for oneself in ways that would have been unacceptable in our families or cultures of origin. The anxiety we carry can easily turn to rage when a person inadvertently disregards a boundary we've recently recognized, especially if we struggled hard to work up the courage to tell them about it once already. This is where the habit of listening sessions can come in handy. Ask to be listened to for five minutes and vent your feelings of anxiety, frustration, and rage *without blaming the other person*. If you fear you won't be able to exercise such restraint, make sure the person paying attention to you is not the person you are upset with. The intensity of your feelings in this situation almost certainly comes from your past history, and it can be a relationship-saver to be able to release those feelings before you are compelled to act them out by attacking your friend or letting them smolder poisonously inside. Then go back and talk to your friend about the boundary you want to establish.

It can be effective to ask your friends to assist you with the boundaries you need to set. Most people resist restrictions on their behavior but accept them willingly when they are doing so as a means of providing assistance for someone they care about. Some people find this approach especially useful in situations where there is not enough time to get a listening session and gain clarity on the boundary that was overstepped. You might say something like, "I'm having a hard time with what just happened here. I don't know exactly what I want, but I'm feeling _____, and I need something to change. Can you help me out with this?"

Vulnerability and emotional honesty takes courage—more courage, in fact, than reactively attacking your "opponent." By taking responsibility for your emotional reactions instead of blaming other people for "making you feel bad," you reverse the most common boundary violation many of us experienced as children. Childhood abuse often comes at the hands of out-of-control parents who make their children believe that they deserve mistreatment because they made their parents angry. By taking responsibility for your own feelings, you break this abusive cycle.

When you learn to count on yourself to set and enforce healthy boundaries, the safety thus developed over time will allow you to achieve a level of intimacy and trust with other people that will transform your life. In the next chapter we'll explore another factor essential for healthy relationships.

Illusionary Self,
Illusionary Other

"You've really got a hold on me"

SMOKEY ROBINSON

I'd like you to start this chapter by doing a short experiment. Relax, get comfortable, close your eyes, and imagine that you are about to meet someone you have never met before. His name is Joe. What is he like? Describe him in detail—how he dresses, what he looks like, what he does for a living, what he does for fun, his basic personality traits. Have fun. Let your imagination have free rein and then say good-bye.

You are about to meet another person you have never met before. His name is Philip. Let your imagination go and describe this man in detail. How does Philip dress and act? What does he do for a living or for fun?

Is Philip different in any way from Joe or is he exactly the same? Most likely you saw a different image. What characteristics did you apply to Joe that you did not apply to Philip? Isn't it curious that a mere name would conjure up such different associations? Imagine if I had told you some other small detail such as the person's race or class background or if I had chosen a name from an obviously different ethnic origin.

The phenomena you have just experienced is called "projection" because the mental process you used involves projecting one's associative inner world of memory, symbolism, and imagination on a limited amount of input from the outside. Projection is something we all do. Our brains are designed to record all kinds of details and make associations from past experiences that enable us to make decisions in the present. For example, if you ate a red berry from an unidentified bush as a child and immediately got sick, you would associate red berries with illness until you acquired enough information to be able to distinguish between the different fruits. We do this in every aspect of our lives, sometimes consciously but more often without conscious awareness. Growing up, we have met many Joes and Philips and have seen images of Joes and Philips in movies and on television. Those images are recorded and become reactivated every time we meet a new Joe or Philip until we reject the associations as inappropriate to this new situation. Generally speaking, these associations are harmless and are automatically shed in light of conflicting information but if an association has a strong emotional charge connected with it or is reinforced by societal conditioning, then the task of removing our projections requires a conscious effort. The deeper this emotional wounding goes, the more difficult and complex the task becomes; but if creating healthy relationships and communities is important to you this is probably the most important work you could do.

PROJECTIONS FROM OUR PAST

There are several common forms of projection that we will examine in this chapter. The first is when a person or current situation reminds us consciously or unconsciously of a person or experience from our past. I had an experience of this just last night. I make part of my living as a graphic designer and recently started a new project that requires working with input from several people at once. One of the members of this group was pressing me to do something that overstepped my professional boundaries and would not listen to my calmly stated objections to his idea. I handled the situation diplomatically but left the meeting feeling furious. I found myself rehearsing angry confrontations with this individual, whom I saw as completely self-centered, immature, and insensitive, and could not shake the experience off. Finally I realized my reaction was not about him at all—it was due to a buildup of frustration about clients insisting I do things I warned them would not work and then being unhappy with the results. I recently made the decision to turn away any work that put me into this position again, but I really wanted this particular job. When I realized where my feelings actually originated, I stopped seeing my "opponent" in such a negative light. He was simply attached to what he thought was a great idea and was eager to have the group adopt it. My highly critical impression was a projection that came through the distorted lens of my inner frustration. Now I'm aware that I neglected to state my boundaries clearly and see that my own pattern of being diplomatic at all costs was trapping me in a position of either accepting unacceptable work conditions or turning away work I want to do. I'm in a more powerful position to change this situation now that I can see the dynamics involved more clearly.

If you have a difficulty in your relationship with someone, the first step toward untangling your feelings and regaining clarity is to ask yourself whom they remind you of or what the situation reminds you of. Trust your first thought no matter how outlandish it might seem at first. How are these two people or incidents similar? Describe every similarity you can think of—the behaviors involved, the style of speech used, the looks, style of dress, age, race, class, or ethnicity of the person you are in disagreement with. If there is some unresolved issue between you and an earlier person, you could use a listening session to say what you needed to say or to work with the emotions in some other way. Many times, however, just bringing to awareness the past issues that are playing themselves out in current relationships is enough to break their hold and allow fresh insights and approaches to emerge.

scribble art

For this exercise you will need paper and a pencil and pen or two different color pens. It is designed to project images very quickly that symbol-
ically represent active influences in your consciousness at a given point in
time. If you repeat this exercise several times over the course of a few
weeks, you will see quite clearly how your state of mind affects your perception of reality. It can be quite illuminating.

1. Using a pencil or a lightly colored pen, scribble randomly on a
piece of paper for a few seconds. Don't worry about what it looks
like (close your eyes if that helps). Just let your hand move anyway it feels like moving until you feel finished.

2. Now breathe deeply and slowly and look at your scribble. Do you
see an image or scene in it? Turn it around and examine it from
other angles until the lines start to suggest some kind of picture.
It helps to relax and free yourself from seeing anything in particular. Your mind automatically attempts to make associations all
the time. Allow it to do so and an image will present itself.

3. When you can see the image, take a darker color pen and trace
the image that you see. If you saw more than one, choose your
first thought. Don't worry if you don't use the entire scribble or
if your lines don't match the scribbled ones or if your result is
less than artistic. The point is to make it possible for someone
else to see the image the scribble suggested to you and to have
a record of it for future reference.

4. Share your drawing and any thoughts you have about it with
your listening partner.

5. Some people want to repeat this exercise right away at least two
or three times. Go ahead. Sometimes a theme starts to present
itself when several scribbles are done in a row.

(continued)

scribble art (continued)

I started doing these scribbles to loosen up my creativity at work. Over time I noticed something interesting. The scribbles I did one day were all sweet and rounded, showing a happy puppy, a tiny child running with a kite, a mother hugging her child. Another day the images were grotesque— distorted frightening faces, a threatening Ninja turtle, a dog having a temper tantrum, a person trapped by a giant hand. I laughed when I realized how the images on the second day reflected the anxious, irritable state I was in. I clearly saw the world differently when I felt that way! Another time I saw a progression in the images I drew. I started with a picture of a sad and dejected person sitting slumped over with her legs crossed. I ended with a fat, serenely smiling buddha in an upright lotus position.

TRYING TO FILL UNFILLABLE NEEDS

The second type of projection is based on a particular kind of childhood hurt that leaves us hungry to fill a need that did not get met adequately when we were young.

We all have a real need for food, air, water, sleep, physical affection, communication, and giving and receiving love. As young children we were totally dependent on the adults around us to meet these needs on a regular basis. When those needs were not met, an experience of hurt was recorded that includes all the feelings and erroneous messages present at the time of the initial experience: feelings of loss, loneliness, powerlessness, despair, deprivation, anger, or longing. When a real need in the present brings up these recorded feelings, we feel it very intensely. It can seem as if our very survival is at stake because at one time, in fact, it was. We are, therefore, pulled to do everything we can to fill those needs, to eliminate those powerfully disrupting feelings. Unfortunately, recorded needs cannot be filled in the present moment; they can only be released.

This is a difficult concept to incorporate—we do, after all, have real ongoing needs. How do we distinguish between present day concerns and recorded ones? This is where the process of projection comes in.

Adults can fill real needs. If we're hungry, we can cook dinner; if we want physical affection, we can ask for a hug; if we are single and lonely, we can join social groups, write a personals ad, or ask our friends to introduce us to someone new. Recorded needs, however, always include the feelings of dependency, hopelessness, and power-lessness we had as dependent young children. When in the grip of this brand of illusion, we compulsively wait for some external someone to make us feel safe or loved or powerful or fulfilled, and we focus on try-ing to get our needs met by that someone instead of taking responsi-bility for filling them ourselves. Projection takes the form of "At last! There's the person who could love me the way I want to be loved." When your energy is obsessively directed towards getting a specific someone to love you in a particular way, you are in the grip of a recorded need.

Recorded needs can also be recognized by their tendency to make people act in addictive ways. They need more and more of their favorite "fix"—love, sex, or food, perhaps—to feel okay about themselves and the world. Without it they feel powerless, unable to cope, unable to focus on what is good about their lives, unable to act in a relaxed, flexible fashion in filling their real needs. This addic-tion can wreak havoc in a relationship. If you are always trying to make the other person in a relationship feel good and it takes more and more energy to do that, you have probably fallen under the spell of a projected recorded need.

A tricky aspect of working with recorded needs in relationships is that patterns have a way of finding their complement. A person with a recorded need to get love ("I'm so needy") is often attracted to a person who has a recorded need to give love ("I need to be needed"). So if you recognize a recorded need in your partner, it's useful to take a look at yourself to see whether you have patterns that are hooking with theirs. You'll have a lot more success unraveling a relationship problem if you concentrate on releasing and acting outside of your own patterns than if you concentrate on getting the other person to change or work on theirs.

role reversal

This is a fun way to unhook patterns that develop between two people, especially if you are in a conflict. Switch roles! Pretend to be your friend and have them pretend to be you and continue to argue from the other person's position. The illusionary nature of the patterns we get into with each other soon becomes apparent.

I sometimes do three-way listening sessions with friends who want to work on their relationships with each other with a third person present. In one instance the wife had a recorded need for physical affection and felt lost and needy without it. Her husband came from a relatively unaffectionate family. He felt close enough at arm's distance and found her desire for more closeness oppressive. When I asked them to play at switching roles, he tried to smother his wife with affection while she acted aloof and held him off. The three of us began to laugh, and it helped the couple see outside of their entrenched positions.

Using Listening Sessions to Work on Recorded Needs

1. Say good-bye to ever filling that past need. Talk about what you missed and allow yourself to grieve or to be angry. Grieving is very important. Many of us believe we gave up the wish to fill these needs long ago only to find that when the "right" person comes along (for instance, a person who reminds us of one of our parents or someone who fits the image of who our ideal parent would have been), we try to fill the needs through a relationship with him or her. Grieving allows us to truly let go,

and frees us to create relationships based on self-respect and reciprocity instead of dependency and lack.

2. Be the parent, friend, etc. you didn't have for yourself. Make taking care of your real needs a priority. Take responsibility for asking for what you want instead of waiting and hoping, manipulating situations, or demanding that your partner fill them for you. For example, you can ask a friend to give you a hug or listen to you when you are sad.

Be sure to take the time to establish what your recorded needs are, even if you do not choose to release the feelings. Increased awareness can go a long way, and completely healing this kind of trauma is not easy. It takes persistence, perhaps even a lifetime of effort, pulling back projections, releasing emotions, and learning new behaviors. This is one area where a listening partner or a very responsive mate is essential. Nobody wants to feel this level of pain by themselves. It feels too hopeless because it happened at such a young age. You need a voice from the outside who will remind you that the hopelessness is a recording and will encourage you to persist and remind you of your goodness and capability of providing for your real needs now.

PROJECTIONS OF LIGHT AND SHADOW

I once used a listening session to work on the runaway feelings I had for a man to whom I was very attracted. My listening partner asked me to tell her what I loved about him and I described a long list of traits. As I was talking I noticed her eyes filling with tears. When I asked why she was crying she said it was because I had just described myself. I replied that I didn't think anything I had said applied to me, and she responded, "That's why I'm crying."

Jungian analysts like to talk about what they call the "shadow," the vast part of our subconscious that contains aspects of ourselves that we do not accept. These are the characteristics that our families, societies, or personal experiences trained us to reject, such as aggression or overt sexuality, but it also contains qualities we label positive that we erroneously believe do not apply to us, such as lovability or creativity. When we meet someone we are especially attracted to, it is very common to project those desirable qualities onto them. Of course, this is not pure projection because the other person may very well embody these characteristics already, but often we think we see these qualities regardless of whether or not they are exhibited. It is also common to reject certain individuals because we project what we consider certain undesirable characteristics onto those people who act in ways we don't permit ourselves. For example, in the story I told earlier about my graphic design project, I projected the characteristics of self-centeredness, immaturity, and insensitivity onto my difficult client. These are all qualities I reject in myself. I pride myself on my professionalism and in my ability to cater unselfishly to my clients' needs. I would feel embarrassed to act the way this man was acting. Yet I could benefit by reclaiming one of the positive aspects of the behaviors he was exhibiting—the ability to put my concerns in the foreground and fight for what I want. If I could learn to embrace my own "self-centeredness," I would be less bothered by his and more able to protect my own boundaries.

working with subpersonalities

C. G. Jung noticed that constellations of related patterns tend to act like separate personalities or "subpersonalities" in the psyche. He believed that acting as if they were separate personalities and engaging with them on that basis would bring them into conscious awareness where they were less likely to interfere negatively in our lives or be projected onto others. By engaging in active dialogue with these aspects of ourselves we can reintegrate them in a healthy way and increase our ability to respond to new situations with flexibility. Examples of common subpersonalities include the Critic, the Rebel, the Inner Child, and the Saint. It is possible to use a listening

(continued)

session or journal to work with subpersonalities. After exploring the first question, step into the role of the subpersonality you want to understand better. Answer the following questions with your first thought:

1. What difficulties does this part bring to your life?
2. Where did you (the subpersonality) come from? What time of your life or set of incidents?
3. What positive qualities do you (the subpersonality) possess? How would integrating these qualities be helpful?
4. What do you want? (Don't censor yourself—say whatever pops into your mind!)
5. What do you need?

Sometimes the answer to question 4 is something you could never allow without detrimental effect. This answer might indicate compulsions you struggle with or actively resist. The answer to question 5 usually indicates a way that you could take care of yourself better. Try to find a way to meet these needs whenever possible and the compulsions will fade.

SOCIETALLY INFLUENCED PROJECTIONS

Projections become even more insidious in situations where we have been societally trained to think of another person as different from us in some fundamental way. Racism is a prime example of this. We make snap judgments about people all the time, especially in situations where our safety or well-being may be at stake. When another race is involved, skin color automatically becomes one of the criteria on which we make decisions, at least on the subconscious level. Our decision-making process includes nonracist personal experience that no sane person would overlook, but racist hearsay, media depictions, and personal history can have a heavy influence. Racism is a complicated issue, but removing projections will help us make informed decisions instead of acting on guilt or unwarranted fear.

When it comes to working with diversity, the task of removing projections belongs to everyone. Don't make the mistake of thinking that your stance of taking the moral high ground or that your status as a member of a disadvantaged group has made you immune from this problem. We're *all* affected by the process of projection, especially when we have learned to reject aspects of our inherent nature, or when we have experienced oppression. When we censor our thoughts, feelings, and behavior to avoid being racist, sexist, or homophobic, our societal conditioning might present itself in less obvious but equally subversive ways. When we have been victimized, pain and fear sometimes distorts our perception of reality by keeping us focused on potential threats that may or may not exist. Furthermore, even positive projections can be harmful because any expectation based on assumptions about a particular group will keep you from seeing clearly the unique human being in front of you.

A friend recently told me that if you go for a walk looking for litter and filth, you will see litter and filth, but if you walk through the world looking for beauty, you will see a beautiful world. Neither perception is fully accurate. The world contains both ugliness and beauty. For me, it is clear that every culture, race, and class has a view of reality that includes both painful illusion and brilliant clarity. We all stand to gain by learning to recognize and pull back projections that keep us from learning from one another's experience. We'll explore more ways to work with societal conditioning in the next chapter.

removing sexist, racist, and other societally conditioned projections

I suggest doing the following exercise in a listening session with someone who will agree to work on the same issue in their turn. It is very difficult to look at the sexist, racist, homophobic, or anti-Semitic attitudes we have unconsciously adopted. Nobody wants to think of themselves as deserving these labels, yet we all grew up in a society riddled with unflattering depictions of various groups of people. These descriptions influence our psyches as young children when we do not have enough information to know better.

1. Choose a group that neither you or your listening partner belong to (for example, men, women, gay, straight, black, white, Jewish, Southern Baptist, etc.).

2. Say the name of the group and then answer the question "What is your first thought connected in any way with this group?" The response might be either a memory or a descriptive word or phrase.

3. Answer the question several times. You might have both positive and negative responses.

4. If memories come up, choose the earliest one and work with the emotional content in any of the ways described earlier in the book.

5. If you have a list of descriptive adjectives, choose a negative one and try to find words that describe positive qualities of the same attribute. For example, a woman might have associated the word "violent" with men. She knows that not all men are violent, but her past experiences create that association. Positive aspects of the word "violent" might be "powerful" or "unrestrained."

(continued)

removing sexist, racist, and other societally conditioned projections (continued)

Then try those descriptions on for yourself. For example, you might say, "I'm powerful! Nothing holds me back!" Say any first thoughts that come up. How do your life circumstances keep you from embodying even the most positive attributes of this characteristic? How does your upbringing differ from the group you ascribed that characteristic to? Is there anything you could learn from the other culture or subgroup? Every negative stereotype is based partially on observed behavior—the problem is that, in addition to having actual hurtful experiences, outside groups tend to misinterpret behavioral patterns that are not common for their own group. For example, I think my next door neighbor is too loud and have judged him very harshly for it; but when I traveled to the country he grew up in, I discovered that most people there speak and play music as loudly as he does. In that setting the very same music seemed passionate and festive. I still want him to turn his stereo down—the noise hurts my ears and keeps me from enjoying the quieter music I play—but I also see how my more restrictive cultural mores keep me from enjoying the same choices he makes

Going Beyond
Societal Boundaries

"Men are close to one another by nature.
They diverge as a result of repeated practice."

CONFUCIUS

What does it take to change the world? Commitment? Dedication? Hard work? How about selfishness? In my experience the most effective world changers are people who are selfishly dedicated to healing their relationship with people of a particular group—women who are fed up with being terrified of men, environmentalists who are tired of fighting with lumberjacks or corporate chairpeople, people of color who refuse to accept second-class status in their relationship with white people, anyone who hates the illusions that keep them separate from anybody else. Gay, straight, black, white, gentile, or Jew, we all stand to gain from learning how to reach across societally conditioned barriers to closeness and harmony.

When I went to the NGO Forum during the Fourth World Conference for Women in Beijing, China, I saw amazing alliances being forged between groups that would never ordinarily choose to work together. What bonded us as a group had nothing to do with ethnic origin, race, or class—we were all women working together for world peace and improving economic and social conditions, not just for ourselves but for all people everywhere. Our roles as the mothers of sons, the wives of husbands, and the daughters of fathers kept us aware of the importance our own liberation could play in improving the health and well-being of our whole societies. I saw more clearly than ever that liberation work is not the self-centered raving of special interest groups, as certain elements of our government and media would have us believe. All liberation work leads to human liberation.

---

the interconnectedness of global problems

Separately or with other people name the big and small, local and global problems operating in the world today and write them on a piece of paper in random order. When the paper is full, look at them in silence for a few minutes. Then notice which problems are connected to each other. If you are with other people, you could discuss this together. Draw arrows between the topics to make the connections visible. Continue drawing arrows until you can no longer think of any more connections. It is highly unlikely that any one topic will stand on its own, unrelated to anything else.

Now think about the issues you care most deeply about and notice the arrows attached to it. Sometimes people think that their pet concerns are insignificant, that this particular "ism" is more important than that one, or that focusing on improving an area that affects us personally is overly selfish. Hopefully, now you can see that working on any one problem will affect every other. Celebrate the significance of your own calling and make a commitment to never denigrate the causes that you are drawn to ever again or to criticize anyone else's choices for activism.

The other quality essential to being an effective world changer is the desire to be a good friend. Why do I say that? A friend of mine who works with the National Coalition Building Institute says you can't change a person's mind, but you can help them have a change of heart. Anything is possible when the appropriate human connections are made. This calls to mind using the "old boy network." The same concept of people helping each other create the wealth they desire can be applied to creating the real wealth of a sustainable, just, and prosperous economy and a peaceful, flourishing environment and social system. What I refer to in this case, however, is not the self-centered networking involved in working a room with a pocketful of business cards. I propose making real friendships genuine enough to inspire acts of generosity and goodwill.

What makes a good friend? Patience, a willingness to listen and to share, a desire to help each other live happy, fulfilling lives, unconditional love and support, and a desire to have fun together. We all want that in our lives and we are all capable of it to varying degrees. So, theoretically, we all have what it takes to be world changers—if you believe that's what it takes. But if it were really so easy, what are we waiting for? Why haven't we done this already? I'll tell you why I hesitate. I immediately think, "But I don't know the right people." And if I did know the "right" people, what comes up next are all the places where I feel inadequate, put down, not good enough, likable enough, or desirable as a friend or ally; all the places where I have been rejected in the past and fear rejection in the future; the places where I was told I must not venture, I must not step on those toes, bother those people, or impose my annoying presence on somebody else's well-ordered existence. How could I, the environmental activist, ever even entertain the possibility of being accepted by a corporate bigwig, never mind being allowed to get past his or her secretary?

We have all heard that where there is a will there is a way, but most of the time, when it comes to making friends outside of our usual circle, our will gets in our way. "I *will* not humiliate myself again," we say. "I *will* not allow myself to be hurt or rejected again. I *will* not be ridiculed. I *will* not be disappointed." Multiply those feelings by 100 percent if the potential friend is someone we think is better than us or different in some significant way.

The place to start, therefore, is NOT where you might think you *should* focus your attention in order to change the world—you can't successfully swim if you're still afraid to jump in the water—but in your own family or established circle of friends. What are the power dynamics that prevent true intimacy right there? I know what you're thinking: She's crazy, what is that going to do? But remember I said *start* at home, don't stay there. What gets in the way of being completely close and committed to your family, your friends, your co-workers, and acquaintances? Age differences? Gender? If making friends there is the challenge you wish to set for yourself, the generation gap in your own family is no less significant than what you will encounter in the halls of corporate America. How could you bridge those gaps?

You start by listening. You must be willing to listen to the ways growing up in this society has affected that person. We are all affected differently, depending on our age, race, class, gender, sexual orientation, religion, etc., because each of these differences is the excuse for different forms of societal oppression.

THE INTERNALIZATION OF SEXISM, RACISM, AND OTHER SOCIETAL OPPRESSIONS

How does societal oppression affect children? Contrary to popular belief, I do not believe that the various "isms" are primarily internalized through blatant discrimination in the marketplace or from media depictions. It happens most often at home and is enforced on the playground by children too young to know the difference between black and white, Jew and Gentile. It comes through ridicule of *any* behavior that seems different from the group's norm. It happens when a child wears white socks with sandals in California or a cowboy hat outside of Phoenix. It happens when a girl finds out she'll catch cooties if she plays with the boys in first grade and when a boy is called a sissy for playing with dolls. It happens when two straight girls hold hands in Massachusetts and are called "lesboes" or when a black child is left out of the ballgame without any racial epithets being used. It's when the fat kid is ridiculed in the lunchroom or when the classroom bully is allowed to torment more sensitive children. Every perceived difference is fair game. We have all experienced discrimination in one form or another. Many people point at racism as the biggest problem facing our society today, but from my perspective the only difference between racism and every other ism is that white children can often learn to protect themselves by conforming, but a black child can never change the color of his or her skin.

Having the option to conform confers a great amount of economic and social benefit, but I would hesitate to call it a blessing or even a privilege. The word "privilege" feels insulting to me as a white person because I have become painfully aware of what I gave up when I was forced to accept that "privilege." Please allow me the opportunity to illustrate a very important point with what might seem like an insignificant example.

When I went to the NGO Forum, I had a moment of envy when I saw the Haitian women celebrating the event wearing colorful clothing made of cloth of their own design. In America their attire would seem outlandish, an outfit suitable only for Halloween, but they wore it with so much style and grace and obvious pride that all the white women around me were awestruck. Today as I write these words I feel sad. I want to walk proudly, too, but the conditioning is so heavy that I wanted to censor this sentence before I even wrote it down. I didn't even want to admit my desire to be flamboyant for fear some well-meaning friend would challenge me to do it.

I remember when I was a child my mother always picked out my clothes. When I finally got old enough and wise enough to insist on making my own selections, I had already learned that I could not choose what I liked. It was certain to lead to ridicule and humiliation because I liked creative glittery outfits full of bright colors, ribbons, beads, and feathers, but my classmates only wore jeans and T-shirts, with plaid overshirts and sweaters added in the winter. So that's what I chose whenever possible, too. I was no fool. Even when I did choose to stand out from the crowd, I did so by becoming a member of a subgroup with its own unspoken rules of conformity. Today I have a closet filled with clothing I still never wear in my original hometown without embarrassment, but which helps me feel right at home in my chosen city of Santa Cruz. Is it what I would choose in the absence of societal pressure to conform? I have no idea. A big part of me says it's not important (how could I be so insensitive as to write about fashion in a chapter about racism or other societal oppressions)? But it's symbolic of something I myself can barely grasp consciously, and I hope you will understand.

All our lives we are told how to walk, talk, live, dress, what to eat, when to eat it, etc., etc., to the extent that very few people in America today have any idea of who they are and what they are capable of being. The soul's message is completely buried beneath thick layers of unimportant rules accepted through intimidation. How many people listen to their internal guidance on a regular basis? How many people march to their own drummers á la Henry David Thoreau, regardless of how important his writing is deemed in the public school system? How many people stand up to oppression when they see it, *if* they can see it through the blinders their own socially-dictated conformity created for them. The clothing we choose to wear is just the tip of the iceberg.

A new ism needs to be coined, and it is the mother of all isms— the ism of difference. We all suffer from it. Racism is simply the most blatant example. It seems like white people are getting more self-centered and less concerned about ending racism, with all their protesting about reverse discrimination and attempts to dismantle affirmative action. But I believe there is a genuine glimmer of hope in these angry displays. White people are starting to notice the ways in which they have been victimized by this society, the ways that they have accepted an inner feeling of powerlessness and an obsession with conformity in exchange for a false sense of security and external positions of power. Now that this security is starting to collapse, programs that give disadvantaged people a hand seem threatening and unreasonable. Eventually, someone is bound to notice that affirmative action does not limit white people's lives nearly as much as do the social conditions that require a soul to give up his or her authority, that interfere with a person's ability to think for him- or herself, and that make it difficult to make choices that come from the heart instead of from fear of poverty or abuse.

MY PROGRAM FOR LIBERATION FROM OPPRESSIVE SOCIAL CONDITIONING

Step 1:

Recognize that the conditioning exists. First of all, ask questions of friends and relatives within your own group(s). What is it like to have grown up a woman in your generation and culture? What is it like to have grown up a man? What is it like to be a black person in a white-dominated culture, to be Jewish in a gentile-dominated culture, etc.? What is it like to be a white gentile? What are the advantages? What have you and your people given up?

Step 2:

Notice the ways that you have internalized messages about your group(s). When you think about other members of your tribe, what do you feel embarrassed or ashamed about? What do you hate about them? Do you cringe around people who fit the stereotypes promoted about your group? In what ways have you learned to reject or change your own behavior?

Step 3:

Take pride in yourself as a member of your group. What's great about being who you are? If you are a member of a minority or subgroup, it is especially important to take pride in those characteristics that the dominant groups label as negative. For example, I grew up hearing that Jews are too loud, too pushy, too intellectual, too emotional, and too obsessed with money, and I cringe when I meet Jews who act like those stereotypes or when I find myself acting in those ways. But from a point of view of pride, I celebrate my Jewish passion about life. I am happy when I allow myself to be vocally unrestrained. I'm proud that my parents encouraged me to be fully engaged in whatever piqued my curiosity. It is enjoyable to learn as much as possible about anything that interests me, including other people, and I don't understand why anyone would deny themselves the pleasure of being as close emotionally to another person as they possibly can. I'm proud of my ambition and expertise in earning enough money not only to take care of my basic needs but to buy the free time I require to live as I choose. I'm proud to come from a culture that is committed to ending social injustice. In Step 2, I focused on legitimate gripes I have about members of my group. In this session, I forgive my people for their failings in living up to their own high standards. Like all other groups, we are perfectly human. Not only that, we have made many positive contributions to this society and have even more to offer.

Step 4:

What is it like to be a member of a group you do not belong to? Ask questions and really listen to the answers. This can be challenging. If you are a member of a dominant group, listening to a person who has experienced discrimination can bring up feelings of guilt for the actions of your group, your ancestors, or yourself. You might also feel angry about your own unacknowledged experiences of victimization. It is even more difficult for people who have grown up with blatant discrimination to listen with open-minded compassion to members of the dominant group. But to outgrow one's role as a victim it is necessary to see how societal oppression limits everybody's lives, albeit in drastically different ways.

Step 5:

Decide to be an ally for members of a group you do not belong to. The balance for seeing oneself as either an oppressor or as a victim is to take on the role of ally because the position of ally is one of both wholeness and power. What does this mean? Notice the ways that your upbringing helps you see outside the illusions that your friends' upbringings create for them, and then actively decide to be supportive in these areas. For example, my conditioning as a Jew makes me feel unwelcome and more than a little paranoid in social situations. I have a few people who have decided to be allies for me in this area. When I'm obviously caught in this particular illusion, they remind me of how much they love having me in their lives, or they make gentle jokes about the "dangerous" people in the room.

I, on the other hand, decided to be an ally to men. I was victimized quite badly by several men in my life. Working directly on this victimization did not help me get beyond it because our society is so full of reminders of the unequal status of women that I could not see that my present life was significantly better than the periods of my life when I experienced the abuse. My fear was so great that I would not be alone with a man even in a professional setting and I had no male friends except for my husband, who decided to be an ally to me. Being afraid of half the human race was completely unacceptable so I decided to rectify the situation by learning everything I could about how boys are conditioned to be men in this society. I found a man who wanted to have a listening partnership with me and little by little learned how to counsel him effectively. I taught peer-counseling classes and insisted that half the class members be male (pretty much unheard of in a setting where 85–90 percent of the participants had been female). Eventually, over a long period of time, I found myself in the position of leading a group where all the participants were men. I remember looking around, marveling at how safe and powerful I felt. My old fears can still be triggered easily enough in certain situations—I can't say I'm completely over this—but this aspect of my life is better than I ever imagined for myself and continues to improve all the time.

Step 6:

Consider making your alliances reciprocal. If you're a woman, you know where men are stuck (we complain about it all the time!); if you're a man, you know where women are stuck. Therefore, we are naturally the perfect people to be allies for one another. Making alliances reciprocal eliminates perceived power imbalances. If you are always in the position of being helped, you always feel less capable than the person who is doing the helping. On the other hand, it is important to be thoughtful about reciprocity. It is powerful for a member of an oppressed minority to decide to be in the role of ally for their own sake; but it can feel oppressive for a member of the dominant culture to insist on it because oppressed groups have historically been forced into being helpmates for the dominant society. The kind of help an ally provides is very different, of course—in fact, there are times when being a great ally means insisting that your partner stretch in ways they would not ordinarily do on their own. In a mutual alliance you would expect your allies to help you stretch as well.

Taking these steps is guaranteed to bring uncomfortable feelings to the surface. It will make all the difference in the world if you can create a safe place to work on feelings that come up for you in being an ally that is separate from your relationship with that person. For example, if you are a black person, the unaware racism of your white friends can be infuriating; yet even the most dedicated white ally will have times when they cannot listen effectively to your anger and pain, especially if you direct it at them. In addition to feeling guilty and bad about themselves, many white people are brought up with strong prohibitions about expressing anger. Sometimes anger is never expressed in their families unless it is accompanied by physical abuse. It can, therefore, be terrifying for white people to be the target of even justifiable and consciously expressed anger. Conversely, if you are white, your black friend may wish you to admit to the racist conditioning you were brought up with but then find it painful to actually listen to the details of your experience with compassion and understanding.

It will be important for both of you to eventually go beyond your limitations because people in polarized groups are naturally the best allies for one another if they get past their own feelings of inadequacy. For example, black people can be good allies for white people by helping them recognize and take pride in their goodness and by supporting them to reclaim a healthy relationship with anger by standing up to oppression. White people can be allies to black people by learning to recognize racial injustice and taking active steps to eliminate it, making it easier for their black friends to release their hopelessness about the white race. In the meantime, it can be useful to have somewhere else to tell your stories and vent your full feelings. Support groups can be the ideal environment for this kind of work because listening to other people working through similar difficulties can be comforting, inspirational, and informative. See the next chapter for information on creating your own world changer's support group.

Community Building

"A single bracelet does not jingle."

CONGO PROVERB

Even though I have spent most of my life studying human relations and have been a staunch proponent of community, I hesitate to begin this chapter. When I think of community I immediately think of the limited relationships I have with my next door neighbors. Privacy is such a high value these days that I haven't lived next to people who wanted to be good friends since I was six years old. There are times when I think we live together well enough. Despite my desire to be great friends with everybody I know, there is a lot to be said for learning to simply live side by side. On the other hand, most people tend to flourish in groups where they feel a sense of belonging and mutual support. Have you ever considered making community-building an intentional act?

Those of us who grew up in the 60s and 70s went about this in a particularly earnest way. Remember the back-to-the-earth commune movement where we idealistically tried to create miniature utopias? We wound up in house meetings that lasted hours while people wrangled over every detail of day-to-day living and processed their feelings about each other ad infinitum. To me, this no longer seems like utopia. Yet, despite the difficulties, I did learn some invaluable skills that have proved useful in creating community in a less intense fashion.

First of all, I learned to give up false expectations about what community actually is. Community is not the perfect family we didn't have when we were growing up. Neither is it the instant fix for the social ills that ail us, or a place where we will feel totally loved and completely connected with other people all the time. There are times when living in community is wonderful and other times when it is a struggle. Most of the time it is somewhere in between.

Second, I learned the importance of listening, which is what this book is all about. In the most intense conflict, the most useful approach is always to listen to your opponent in the most respectful, loving way possible. I have never seen a person who has felt truly heard and understood fail to slow down enough to listen to the other side. Angry people expect an angry response or at least some sort of negative reaction. Stepping back from one's own agenda for a moment and making an honest effort to reach beyond the superficial level of interaction can be a surprisingly disarming act. I'm not a conflict resolution expert—in fact, I hate conflict—but I know that respectful listening works wonders, and I use it whenever possible.

Third, when false expectations are dropped and fear of conflict is diminished, community can be a joyful experience, well worth the effort it sometimes entails. I love community. I love sharing impromptu dinners and planned potlucks, dancing and playing marimba with my African music community, watching videos with my video-watching friends, going on hikes, and doing artwork with others. I like sharing tools and skills with mutual friends, trading computer assistance for sewing, massage for graphic design. I like knowing I can call my friends in a crisis and they can call me in crisis. It is especially important that we have learned the listening skills to provide useful emotional support. I found my friends more useful in one particular crisis in my life than the three professional psychotherapists I called in my panic. It's not that they were better trained, but they loved me without hesitation or fear of breaking a professional boundary. I knew they were on my side and would not let me down no matter how bad things got.

I also like larger experiences of community. My husband participates in a beach clean-up every year, and I helped organize our city's first alcohol-free, family-oriented, New Year's Eve "First Night" celebration. Working together and celebrating together are both activities that make people feel happy and connected. I also discovered firsthand the deep bonding that occurs when people successfully tackle a monumental problem. In the aftermath of the 1989 earthquake here in Santa Cruz there were numerous opportunities for community activism of the most practical kind as well as a need for visionaries who could hold out a hopeful future. The downtown renaissance and community spirit that grew out of these efforts were almost worth the pain of having the buildings fall down around our ears.

Community is a big part of my life, and it can be a big part of yours if you want it.

START YOUR OWN COMMUNITY GROUP

The best way to create community I know is to gather people together for any shared purpose. Any group of people will feel like a community when they are engaged in a joint project with tangible results or when they gather specifically to share emotional support. Within the context of a larger group you will always be able to find a few people whom you can count on to be lifelong friends or whom you could enlist for another concern that is important to you.

Besides joining groups that already exist, it is relatively easy to design your own network of like-minded friends. All you need is three or more people who want to come together on a regular basis for any reason. If you are new to a city or want to find people with a specific interest that your current friends don't share, you can find people by putting a notice in the local newspaper or by posting a flyer at the gym, the library, or local community center. You can create groups based on any hobby or interest, to share information and resources for an unlimited number of purposes, and to build the trust and deep connections necessary to tackle any project or life issue.

Don't think that starting small is a limitation of any sort. If you're having fun, other people are sure to want to join. I know a quilting group that has become so large that they need to rent a church hall every month. They have guest speakers, do day-long workshops, go on field trips, and put on a large quilt fair every year. The quilters who wanted the intimate experience of sharing stories around the quilting frame have formed smaller subgroups of five to eight people that meet between meetings. (Any group that focuses on emotional support works best in this size range.) Some of these small groups have taken on other projects such as providing home-made quilts for the local homeless shelter and volunteering to teach traditional artforms in the public schools. They attend each other's weddings, babysit each other's children, and share potlucks at Thanksgiving and Christmas. A true community has developed from a shared interest in a simple craft.

Once you have the people, you need to decide when you will meet, where, and for how long. If the intention of your group is primarily emotional support, a good rule of thumb is at least 15 minutes of time per person plus an equal amount of time for socializing, announcements, and the business of running the meeting. About three hours seems to be the limit for any kind of regular evening event. How often to meet depends on the needs of your members. A committed ongoing group where the members know each other fairly well or a large hobby-oriented group can meet successfully once a month without losing continuity; but a group coming together for a specific project or a newly formed emotional support group will do better meeting every week. Choose a meeting spot large enough to allow everyone to sit comfortably and private enough to avoid distracting interruptions.

Regardless of the purpose of your meeting, it will go better if there is an expected structure and one person taking charge of making things run smoothly. This can be as simple as saying we're going to meet at Sue's house at such and such a time, Ann's in charge of calling people and providing cookies and tea, and we're going to pull out our sewing and gab; or it can be as complex as having a detailed agenda with set time limits for each item. It is important to allow room for spontaneity and free-flowing social interaction, but without an agreed upon structure facilitated by someone who has taken on the responsibility, meetings can become so chaotic and unproductive that group members get frustrated and stop attending. A group that wishes to empower its members by sharing leadership might take turns filling this role each time.

SPECIAL GUIDELINES FOR SMALL GROUPS

I define a small group as one where everybody knows each other and can fit into a person's living room. This kind of group has special benefits and issues that larger, less familial groups do not share. These are the groups where a strong feeling of community is most likely to develop as well as the kind of setting where problems can create the most pain.

The quality of the attention we share one-on-one is magnified many times over in a small group. If the quality of attention is deficient, problems always develop; if the quality is good, wonderful things can happen. A group is essentially a synergistic system. Whatever you do or do not do has a significant effect. For example, if people have side conversations or flip through papers reading when someone is speaking, a distraction is created that the speaker must actively resist paying attention to or address in some way. The people across the room from the distraction and those on either side are similarly affected. On the other hand, if only one person speaks at a time and everyone else gives that person their full attention, the speaker will be able to relax and concentrate on what he or she is trying to say. If the attention offered by the group is the kind of loving, supportive attention we share in focused listening sessions, this sense of relaxation will be even deeper. The speaker will gain confidence and the quality of what they have to share may even improve.

Synergistic dynamics also become apparent when there is a major disparity in how often each person speaks. Without some attention to group process or without using a relatively tight structure, it is very common for one or two people to dominate the proceedings habitually while others never participate at all. Both of these styles of interaction often seem beneficial to the people using them; however, they both lead to negative results. When some people are habitually silent, other group members start to feel uncomfortable. What are they thinking? Do they approve or disapprove of what's going on? Don't they trust us? When a person acts as though they don't trust the group, the rest of the group may feel untrustworthy or defensive. Conversely, when a few people dominate conversations by interrupting or trying to hurry a person that is having trouble speaking, or by expressing knee-jerk reactions to almost anything anyone else says, they effectively silence other people. Because they act untrustworthy, other members of the group feel and act like the group as a whole cannot be trusted. Safety is thus eroded and resentments flare up in tumultuous ways. It is very important in small groups that everyone receives roughly an equal amount of respectful attention, if not every time then over the course of several meetings. You might take equal turns speaking or assign one person to monitor the interaction level of the group and encourage quiet people to speak and talkative ones to hold back. Some groups pass a "talking stick" or some other object to help group members focus on one person at a time. The person holding the talking stick is the center of attention and everyone else is expected to refrain from interrupting. Setting an informal time limit per person can also be helpful.

It usually feels uncomfortable for some people to impose this much structure. We come from a generation where structure is associated with abusive authority and unreasonable limitations on personal freedom. But structure can also be thought of as a container solid enough to hold the fluidity of personal relationships. If you want to avoid spending more time processing internal dynamics than attending to the issues that brought you together, it is a good idea to use a structure that makes it easy for people to participate thoughtfully, despite any tendency they might have to do otherwise.

Except in unusual circumstances, it is also important to encourage group members to stay focused on the group's intended agenda.

For example, it is very common for people who do not have enough support in one area of their lives to try to use any group they are in as a sounding board for their personal problems. Other people use their speaking time to change the subject to another issue they want the group to address even though no resolution has been reached on the current issue. These habits divert attention from the group's chosen agenda and generate frustration and resentment when it is repeated over a long period of time. Use your meetings as a place to practice healthy boundaries by respecting each other's time and energy. If your personal desire is to create an emotional support network, get together with those people who feel the same and create a group specifically for that purpose.

EMOTIONAL SUPPORT GROUPS

Emotional support groups can never take the place of good friends simply relaxing with each other and sharing each other's lives. However, there are times when we need the more focused attention a listening partnership provides. Creating a small group for using the listening skills presented in this book will take you further than practicing them on your own with one person. It is easier to learn new skills with other people dedicated to the same task. If you and your partner both join the same group, you will have the opportunity to see each other being counseled by people who do not have your particular blind spots or limitations. You can also ask for suggestions from the group about what they would do in a particular counseling situation.

Creating a support group is also useful for working on issues that are particularly challenging. For example, I know a group of white people who started an Eliminating Racism support group. Every person in the group had made a commitment to oppose racism wherever they encountered it but discovered that the most difficult racism to oppose was the unconscious variety they carried themselves. They needed a safe place to uncover these attitudes without fear of attack.

Support groups are especially useful for decreasing feelings of isolation when working on issues that few people share. For example,

I started a Self-Employed Persons group that helped me see that some of my struggles with self-employment were common problems instead of an indication of some unusual deficiency. It helped me drop that particular self-criticism and focus on practical solutions instead of excessive self-improvement.

Another specific use for support groups that I find beneficial is a goal-pursuing group. The group helps each other develop doable steps toward each person's current hopes and dreams. They then help each other take those steps. Each meeting ends with each person making a commitment to do at least one task toward their goal that week. Each meeting begins with a check-in about how each person fared during the week before. Sometimes group members agree to call each other for support during the week as well. Amazing things happen in groups like this. It's very empowering to make progress toward something you care about and inspiring to see other people do so.

An effective format for an emotional support group is a few minutes of free-form socializing when people first arrive, followed by a formal sharing of attention at a prearranged time. Group members might take turns doing short check-ins (1–2 minutes each) about what's going well in their lives or they might answer a question related to the topic of the evening, if there is one. There could be a sharing of information on a topic related to the group's focus by the group leader or a guest speaker, and then the bulk of the time could be split evenly by all in attendance, with one person receiving attention from the entire group at one time. Everyone else would provide the kind of attention given in a focused listening session, meaning they would refrain from giving advice unless asked or from telling their own stories. After everyone has received attention, the group would finish the business of the meeting with short announcements, the date of the next meeting, and choosing the next facilitator. A closing ritual such as a group hug, a song, or a round of appreciations is a good way to end.

appreciation circles

Very few of us ever get appreciated enough. This is a very easy way to generate feelings of belonging or to lift the spirits of someone feeling unloved.

In a circle say something you like about the person on your left or right and go around the circle. Especially effective appreciations might include how knowing this person has made a positive difference in your life.

Variation:

One person at a time stands in the middle of the circle with eyes closed and "overhears" the rest of the group saying good things about them. I've often thought it is too bad that people don't get to hear the eulogies at their funerals before they are dead. This is a way to create a similar experience for the living.

DAY-LONG OR WEEKEND EVENTS

An occasional day-long or weekend retreat or workshop is a fine idea. I like to create such events for the peer-counseling classes I teach. It's a great way for people to get to know each other better, to focus intensely on a particular topic, and to have a lot of fun. At the workshops I lead I include instruction on basic or more advanced counseling skills, demonstrations, a question and answer period, reciprocal practice sessions, and support group meetings. We also have lots of structured and unstructured relaxation times, playtimes, and great meals.

I have also created less formal weekend retreats with friends. One time, two friends and I stayed at a cabin in the woods to focus on changes we each wanted to make in our lives. We did Tarot readings for each other, split listening time, popped popcorn in the fireplace, went on hikes, and cooked wonderful gourmet meals in addition to the usual story-sharing and friendly gossiping. It was a great break from our usual, busy lives.

A weekend workshop requires a fair amount of advance preparation. You will need to find a place large enough and comfortable enough for the size and budget of your group. If someone in your group is in a wheelchair, you will have to check the facility for wheelchair accessibility in advance. Also inquire about sleeping quarters, chairs, an auditorium, a stage, or kitchen facilities, if you need them. If you will be providing meals, you should plan your menu ahead of time and do the shopping. You will also need to plan what you intend to do together and make at least a loose schedule so people will be able to relax and bring any appropriate items. If you want a guest speaker, performer, or teacher, make advance reservations that will fit their needs as well.

A good format for a weekend workshop is to spend Friday night doing introductions, getting-to-know-you exercises, or warm-ups you or the designated group leader for the event deems appropriate. This is the time to set the tone for the rest of the weekend. Is this going to be a silly, free-spirited romp, or a serious get-down-to-business intensive? Is the purpose to deepen your friendships, expand your knowledge, sharpen skills you already have, accomplish tasks, or all of the above? Are there goals you wish to accomplish over the course of the weekend? Friday night is when you set up the expectations and direct the focus for the rest of the event.

Saturday is when you get into the meat of your program. It is important to plan a good mix of activities, both participatory and passive, with adequate breaks for stretching, playing, and relaxing. Don't let people go too long without eating or moving their bodies. Sometime during the day or evening, or at both times, plan a fun activity like dancing, skit-performing, singing, or game playing that will get people into a playful frame of mind. Even the most serious work-oriented gathering will benefit from allowing people to shift their focus occasionally.

Sunday is the day for follow-up of the previous day's activities, tying up loose ends, answering any remaining questions, providing one last practice session or group activity, clean-up, and saying good-bye. Be sure to include a closing ritual that will focus people's attention on what they enjoyed or learned over the weekend and what they look forward to when they get home.

A Few Thoughts on Leadership

"Your playing small does not serve the world.
There's nothing enlightened about shrinking so
that others don't feel insecure around you."

NELSON MANDELA

I like to think of myself as a leader and I hope you do, too, or will soon.

What does it take to be a leader? Being an expert? I hope not. If you assume that an expert is anyone who has written a book, or someone who has mastered all of the issues they talk about, think again. Some people will attempt to call me an expert for writing this book, but I can assure you that few authors are masters at everything they write about. My knowledge comes from positive experience, learning, and study, but perhaps the greatest gifts I'm attempting to share have come from experiences where I have failed many times. I think of myself as a guide walking the same path, perhaps only a few steps ahead. In other circumstances you could be my guide.

Does being a leader mean being the perfect role model? God help me! If I need to go through life now as the perfect peer counselor, I think I'll rip this up and save myself the grief. We are very harsh on our teachers and leaders in this country. We put them on pedestals and expect them to fill the role of the perfect parent or guru we always wanted. When they inevitably show their human failings, we pull them down and drag them through the mud. It's no wonder so few people choose to go into politics or take any role that would put them in the limelight. Grant yourself full permission to make big mistakes, and you'll be a wonderful role model of how to be perfectly human—which is all any leader needs to be.

In my opinion, a great leader is someone who chooses to make things right in the world around them, a person who pays attention to what could go better and takes charge of making it happen. A leader needs only her or his internal prodding to decide to make a difference, and inspires other people to make a difference, too, by soliciting their best thinking and encouraging them to take action. We are all capable of being leaders for each other. If you approach every interaction with the attitude of "what can I learn and what can I share," your interactions will embody the kind of leadership that empowers yourself and others.

I would like everyone to think of themselves as leaders because if everyone were empowered to think for themselves and act responsibly, the problems this world faces would be a lot easier to solve. This cannot happen when people trust those in authority to make all the decisions and initiate all the actions that need to occur. It especially cannot happen when we trust anyone's thinking—no matter how high an authority—over our own. I always tell people not to leave what I say unquestioned just because I am the teacher. I can be wrong. I might not have full information. I always think of a dinner party I attended where the topic of conversation turned to drought tolerant plants. I was telling everybody that my favorite drought tolerant plant was the Peruvian lily because you never have to water them and they continue to stay green and produce flowers all season. Somebody said they never heard of Peruvian lilies being drought tolerant, so I offered to show her my flowers, which I had not watered for three rain-free months. At this my husband burst out laughing. "They're still alive because I water them!" he said. Sheryl, the great gardening teacher, was telling the truth from her experience, but her information was incomplete. We often need to trust our teachers and leaders, but trusting other people does not mean putting aside your own thinking and experience. Always be a leader, at least in your own life, by deciding for yourself what to do and what to think.

With the tools in this book you now have the ability to take charge of your own liberation from painful illusion. This will enable you to take charge of your life and help others do the same. You don't need permission or a special type of relationship to use the listening skills presented here. Take them out any time you want to get to know someone better, any time someone is hurting, any time you need to resolve a conflict or reach across an unintentional boundary. It never hurts to listen with unconditional love. Thinking well about people is what leadership is all about.

Leadership is also choosing to create a world that makes you happy and provides for your highest good. What kind of world would that be? Think about your loftiest goals in every aspect of your life. How do you want your family to be, your friendships, your other relationships? What kind of work would be most fulfilling? What needs to happen for you and your loved ones to be in the best of health? What are your deepest desires for your community, your society, your world? With these greater goals in mind, think about what steps, large or small, you could take to head in that general direction. Break the project into ever-smaller chunks until you have doable steps that would be relatively painless to incorporate into your life. What could you do five years from now, one year, six months, one month, next week, tomorrow? Be a leader in your own life by deciding to pursue your heart's desire, and use your counseling skills to deal with whatever feelings your decisions bring up. If you help other people do the same, you'll inspire each other to heights you cannot imagine. You'll both find that leadership is a joy when it leads to a joyful life. And it is as natural as holding hands while you cross the street.

Have fun!

Recommended Reading and Resources

BOOKS

Blood-Patterson, Peter, ed. *Rise Up Singing*. Sing Out Corporation, Bethlehem, PA., 1988. A songbook with the lyrics of well-known pop and folk songs. A great way to build community spirit, create an event, or pass the time on a long car trip.

Remen, Rachel Naomi, M.D. *Kitchen Table Wisdom: Stories That Heal*. Riverhead Books, New York, 1996. A very enjoyable book about the power of listening.

Shaffer, Carolyn R., and Anundsen, Kristin. *Creating Community Anywhere: Finding Support and Connection in a Fragmented World*. Jeremy P. Tarcher/Perigee Books, New York, 1993. This is the single best book on creating community I have found. It is a valuable resource whether you want to create a simple network of friends or a full-scale cooperative village. It also includes tools for conflict resolution, facilitating meetings, and creating community-oriented celebrations.

Sher, Barbara and Gottlieb, Annie. *Teamworks!* Warner Books, New York 1989. This is a great resource for action-oriented support groups. Very upbeat and inspirational.

Shields, Katrina. *In the Tiger's Mouth: An Empowerment Guide for Social Action*. New Society Publishers, Philadelphia, 1994. An excellent resource for world changers, filled with tools and exercises that can be used in support groups or listening partnerships.

ORGANIZATIONS

Changing Tiger Institute, 317 California Street, Santa Cruz, CA 95060, (408) 469-0714. e-mail: sheryl@changingtiger.com. Website: http://www.changingtiger.com. This is my organization. The name Changing Tiger comes from a passage in the *I Ching*: "The great person changes like a tiger!" It means a great revolution, a triumph of the human spirit.

Changing Tiger Institute is dedicated to helping create such a revolution through joyful empowering tools, ideas, and events. You can contact me through this organization about teaching classes or workshops on Focused Listening for your organization, business, or circle of friends.

Fellowship of Intentional Communitities, Route 1, Box 155-WEB, Rutledge, MO 63563-9720, (660) 883-5545. Website: http://www.well. com/user/cmty/index.html. This organization provides information and access to resources for seekers of community, and for existing and forming communities. They publish the *Directory of Intentional Communities* and *Communities* magazine, both important resources for people interested in intentional community building. Their website is amazing—if this topic is interesting to you, go visit it!

The International Re-evaluation Counseling Communities, 719 Second Avenue, North, Seattle, WA 98111, (206) 284-0311. Web site: http:// www.rc.org. This is a large peer-counseling organization that I have been involved with for 15 years. If you are interested in a less spiritual approach to peer counseling, you may find their information useful. It has especially good publications available about working with societal oppressions, childrearing, and other topics.

National Coalition Building Institute, 1835 K Street, N.W., Suite 715, Washington, D.C. 20006. Website: http://www.ncbi.org. NCBI is a nonprofit, peer-based leadership training organization dedicated to eliminating prejudice and reducing intergroup polarization. There are chapters in major cities throughout the United States, which offer training workshops and programs on prejudice reduction and conflict resolution.

Parents Leadership Institute, P.O. Box 50492, Palo Alto, CA 94303, (650) 424-8687. This is an excellent resource for parents who want to learn to create listening partnerships. Classes and resource groups are available as well as a series of pamphlets on parental listening skills such as dealing with children's crying, anger, or fears. A sample of one of these pamphlets is available on the web at http://www.earlychildhood. com/articles/listen.html.

BOOKS BY THE CROSSING PRESS

Clear Mind, Open Heart
Healing Yourself, Your Relationships and the Planet
By Eddie and Debbie Shapiro

The Shapiros offer an uplifting, inspiring, and deeply sensitive approach to healing through spiritual awareness. Includes practical exercises and techniques to help us all in making our own journey.
$16.95 • Paper • ISBN 0-89594-917-2

Conscious Marriage
From Chemistry to Communication
By John C. Lucas, Ph.D.

What are the tools of effective relating? Why don't we utilize them as we should in relationships? What has caused the cycle of dysfunction that has typified so many marriages in the past few decades? How do we grow beyond it? Lucas provides answers to these questions with a blueprint for building a successful relationship.
$14.95 • Paper • ISBN 0-89594-915-6

Your Body Speaks Your Mind
How Your thoughts and Emotions Affect Your Health
By Debbie Shapiro

Debbie Shapiro examines the intimate connection between the mind and body revealing insights into how our unresolved thoughts and feelings affect our health and manifest as illness in specific parts of the body.
$14.95 • Paper • ISBN 0-89594-893-1

Peace Within the Stillness
Relaxation & Meditation for True Happiness
By Eddie and Debbie Shapiro

Meditation teachers Eddie and Debbie Shapiro teach a simple, ancient practice which will enable you to release even deeper levels of inner stress and tension. Once you truly relax, you will enter the quiet mind and experience the profound, joyful, and healing energy of meditation.
$14.95 • Paper • ISBN 0-89594-926-1

BOOKS BY THE CROSSING PRESS

Pocket Guide to Meditation
By Alan Pritz

This book focuses on meditation as part of spiritual practice, as a universal tool to forge a deeper connection with spirit. In Alan Pritz's words, "Meditation simply delivers one of the most purely profound experiences of life, joy."

$6.95 • Paper • ISBN 0-89594-886-9

Pocket Guide to Self Hypnosis
By Adam Burke, Ph. D.

Self-hypnosis and imagery are powerful tools that activate a very creative quality of mind. By following the methods provided, you can begin to make progress on your goals and feel more in control of your life and destiny.

$6.95 • Paper • ISBN 0-89594-824-9

Pocket Guide to Visualization
By Helen Graham

Visualization is imagining; producing mental images that come to mind as pictures we can see. These pictures can help you relax, assess and manage stress, improve self-awareness, alleviate disease and manage pain.

$6.95 • Paper • ISBN 0-89594-885-0

To receive a current catalog from The Crossing Press
please call toll-free, 800-777-1048.
Visit our Web site on the Internet: www. crossingpress.com